SARA

A PRINCESS

THE STORY OF A NOBLE GIRL

FANNIE E. NEWBERRY

1st WORLD
LIBRARY
Literary Society

Sara, a Princess

Fannie E. Newberry

© 1st World Library, 2006
PO Box 2211
Fairfield, IA 52556
www.1stworldlibrary.com
First Edition

LCCN: 2006935228

Softcover ISBN: 1-4218-2481-7
Hardcover ISBN: 1-4218-2381-0
eBook ISBN: 1-4218-2581-3

Purchase *"Sara, a Princess"*
as a traditional bound book at:
www.1stWorldLibrary.com/purchase.asp?ISBN=1-4218-2481-7

1st World Library Literary Society

Giving Back to the World

"If you want to work on the core problem, it's early school literacy."

- James Barksdale, former CEO of Netscape

"No skill is more crucial to the future of a child, or to a democratic and prosperous society, than literacy."

- Los Angeles Times

Literacy... means far more than learning how to read and write... The aim is to transmit... knowledge and promote social participation."

- UNESCO

"Literacy is not a luxury, it is a right and a responsibility. If our world is to meet the challenges of the twenty-first century we must harness the energy and creativity of all our citizens."

- President Bill Clinton

"Parents should be encouraged to read to their children, and teachers should be equipped with all available techniques for teaching literacy, so the varying needs and capacities of individual kids can be taken into account."

- Hugh Mackay

A Princess she, though not by birth:
Her title's from above,
Her heritage the right of worth,
Her empire that of love.

CONTENTS

CHAPTER I

OMENS, GOOD AND ILL

"Sairay! Sairay!"

The high, petulant voice rose shrilly through the steep, narrow stairway, and seemed to pierce the ears of the young girl who sat under the low, sloping roof, nearly bent double over the book in her lap.

She involuntarily raised both hands to her ears, as if the noise distressed her, then dropped them, straightened herself resolutely, and answered in a pleasant contralto, whose rich notes betokened power and repression, -

"Well, mother?"

"Your fayther's got to hev them nets mended right away, he says, an' my han's is in the dough. Be you at them books agin?"

"Yes," said Sara; "but I'll come," rising with a sigh, and carefully slipping a bit of paper between the leaves of her book, before she laid it on the rough board shelf at one side of the little garret room.

As she passed directly from the stairway into the kitchen, or living-room, her father turned from the hopeless-seeming tangle of soiled and torn netting on the floor before him, and looked at her half wistfully from under the glazed brim of his wide hat.

"Was you studyin', Sairay? Ye see, I've got into a bad sort o' mess here, an' we may git our orders fur the long fish any day."

"That's all right, father! No, baby, sister can't take you now," as the little fellow on the floor crept to her feet and set up a wail; but her smile, and a replaced toy, silenced the cry, and brought back comfort and complaisance to the puckered little face.

Sara then stepped to her father's side, and drew the large soiled fish-net towards her, looking with dismay on the broken meshes; but her voice was still bright, as she said, -

"You must have had a big haul, father, to make such a rent!"

"Waal, 'twas partly thet, but more the ice. Ye see, it's jest breakin' up now, and it's monstrous jagged-like; 'twas thet did it, I reckon. Kin ye fix it, Sairay?"

"Yes, father."

She was soon seated, the dirty mass across her knee, and the large bone shuttle in her hand flying rapidly in and out. But while her young stepmother went and came, talking a good deal, and the baby pulled and scrambled about her knees, her thoughts were far away, in the large schoolroom at Weskisset.

For one short, happy year she had been an inmate of the seminary there, and in her thoughts this year was the Round Top of her life! All events dated from before or since her "school-time." All paths with her led to Weskisset, as with the ancients all roads led to Rome: it was her Athens, her Mecca, almost her Jerusalem.

Sara's own mother, though born inland, had come as school-mistress, some twenty years since, to the little fishing-village of

Fannie E. Newberry

Killamet (now Sara's home), where she was wooed and won by the handsome, honest, daring young fisherman, Reuben Olmstead.

Sara was their first child, and upon her the young mother lavished untold tenderness. When, at the birth of the twins, nearly seven years later, - two infants having died between, - she yielded up her own gentle life, her last words had been, -

"Don't forget, Reuben, that Sara is to have an education. I can see already that she is going to care for books, and she'll need it more than ever, now - promise me, husband!" and the good man would sooner have cut off his weather-beaten spear-hand than break his promise to that dying wife.

In fulfilment of it he had struggled with what, to his fellow-villagers, seemed most foolish persistence, in order to give his oldest child immense and needless advantages, though it had been difficult enough to find the ways and means for these. Even after the usual annual three months of the "deestric" for several years, he had felt that his solemn promise still bound him to allow her at least one year at the seminary.

Nor did the loss of his aged mother, who had been house-keeper since his wife's death, weaken this resolution; and it was, perhaps, partly to make it possible for Sara to leave home, that he had married the young woman of the shrill voice, two years ago. She could look after the house and children while "Sairay got her finishin' off," as he expressed it.

But Sara, like many another scholar, found that her one poor little year was but a taste of wisdom, but one sip from the inexhaustible stream of learning, and, back once more in her childhood's home, was constantly returning to those living waters, with an unquenchable thirst.

It was her stepmother's pet grievance that "Sairay was allers at them books," which was hardly true; for the girl took all the care of her younger brother and sister, and much of the baby, while not a few of the household duties devolved upon her. But she undoubtedly was apt to hurry through her tasks, and disappear within the little attic room above the kitchen in cold weather, or under a certain shady cove down by the sea in summer, as soon as these were finished.

She had been netting but a short time when Morton and Mary came tumbling in, two lively youngsters nearing eleven years, whose bronzed and rosy cheeks betokened plenty of sunshine and fresh air.

"Say, pa!" they cried in a breath, almost stumbling over the baby in their excitement, Mary, as usual, in advance, "is it true you're going out for the long fish to-morrow? Jap Norris told us so on our way home from school."

The father's kindly eyes rested upon them with an indulgent twinkle in their depths.

"Waal, naow, if there's a bit o' news in this hull taown thet you younkers don't pick up, I'd like to find it! Yes, ef Jap Norris said so, I s'pose it's true; he oughter know, bein' as his fayther's the cap'n. How long'll it take to finish up thet air net, darter?"

"Not much longer; but isn't it early to start, father? The ice is hardly broken up, is it?"

"Waal, it's breakin' fast, Sairay; another day or two like this'll fetch it, an' it's 'first come best haul,' ye know, nowadays, sence all creation's got to runnin' to the Banks. Seems like it ain't skurcely fair for them sportin' men to go out jest for fun; they might leave cod an' herrin' to them what makes a business o' catchin' 'em, seems to me; but there, 'tain't so easy to keep a mortgage on the sea!" and he laughed good-humoredly. Meanwhile Molly, as they called the little Mary, had flung off her hood, and now was down on the floor playing with baby Ned, who welcomed her with crows of delight, for when she felt good-natured she was his favorite playmate.

The room would have seemed overflowing to a stranger, with its curtained bed in the alcove - or rather square projection - at one side, its fireplace at the end, and cradle, table, spinning-wheel, reels, and nets, to fill every available space left over.

Even the ceiling was made useful; for along the rafters were hooks which supported spears, oars, and paddles, while one wall was prettily tapestried with a great brown net, its sinkers hanging like ornamental balls along one edge.

The windows were small and the ceiling low, but the fire shone merrily, and gave light, warmth, and cosiness to the crowded apartment.

It was Sara who had pleaded for the restoration of the open fireplace, and the removal of the cook-stove to a bit of shed just back; and though at first the young mother had fretted at the innovation, she found it so much more cheerful, and such a saving of candles in the long evenings, that she had ceased to grumble.

As the night closed in, after their quickly disposed of supper, they all drew closer about the drift-wood fire, and no one, not even Mrs. Olmstead, seemed inclined to talk.

Sara's eyes wandered often from her book to the rugged face of her father, and each time she saw his eyes gazing thoughtfully into the flames.

In fact, the only sound in the room was the sleepy simmer of the water-soaked logs, and an occasional giggle from the twins, who were absorbed in some game which they played with horn buttons on a bit of board, marked off with chalk into the necessary squares. Once the baby gave a sweet, low laugh in the midst of his dreams in the cradle, and then honest Reuben Olmstead turned and smiled towards the little one in a sad fashion, which made Sara feel the tears near.

"Poor little goslin'!" he said tenderly. "Daddy hopes there'll be suthin' for him to do not quite so tough as facin' March sou'-westers; but then, who kin tell? He's a likely little chap, eh, Sairay?"

"Yes, father; he's a dear baby!"

He turned a little, and glanced back at his wife, who stood across the room reeling off twine, and, hitching his chair a trifle nearer the girl, said in a lower voice, -

"Sairay, ef 't should ever happen 't they was left to you to look arter, all three on 'em, would ye be good to the little fellar too, eh?"

"You know I would, father!"

"Waal, waal, yes, I s'posed ye would, Sairay. I really did, naow; only he ain't jest the same to ye as the twins, to be shore, so I jest thort I'd ask, thet's all, Sairay." He nodded at her once or twice in a conciliatory way, then turned back to his fire-gazing for a long moment, after which he rose stiffly, with a half moan of reluctance.

"Waal, s'pose I must go daown to the boats, an' help 'em a while. Guess likely Nick Hornblower ain't good fer much to-night; too much grog aboard, I'm feared. Hand me them boots, sonny."

Morton, having just risen from his game badly worsted by Molly, who could never refrain from taunting her conquered foe, was glad to make a digression by bringing both the hip-boots and a long worsted scarf, as well, and after the father had passed out came to his older sister's side.

He gave the outer log one or two gentle kicks, which sent the sparks flying upwards like a covey of fire-flies, and finally said in a voice too low for Mrs. Olmstead to hear, -

"Sara, I got a licking to-day!"

"Morton! What for?"

"'Cause I sassed the teacher. He don't know beans, Sara, he don't; and I can't help grinning in his face when he tells us things just the opposite of what you do."

"But I may be wrong, Morton. What was it?"

"It's lots of things, all the time. Guess when you tell me a river runs west I ain't a-going to say it runs east, am I? No, sir; not for anybody!"

Sara smiled.

"Well, Morton, we'll have to be pretty sure about things then, won't we? Where's your geography? Let's go over the lesson together. Oh! you're on Russia, aren't you? I was just reading something about that country myself. Think of its being so cold they chop up the frozen milk and sell it in chunks; and they go to bed in a sheepskin bag, which they draw up all about them, and fasten around the neck."

"I'd like that!" laughed the boy. "Tell me some more;" and he dropped upon a low seat, which was simply a square block of wood in the chimney-corner, while Molly, her face all alight with eagerness, joined the group.

These true stories of Sara's were the children's delight; for she had the faculty of making them more interesting than fiction, as she told them in simple, vivid language, with her sweet, full voice, pointed by her intelligent face.

But after a time they were sent off to bed, and Sara was left alone with her mother, who now sat knitting before the fire. The wind had risen outside, and was wailing mournfully around the cottage. The young girl shivered to hear it.

"Sounds like a death-wail, don't it?" said Mrs. Olmstead, noticing the movement. "When the wind hes thet sorter long scream in it, it allers means trouble, and your pa off for the long fish to-morrow!"

She shook her head dismally, and went on in a lugubrious tone, "Besides, didn't ye notice the windin' sheet in the candle las' night, an' didn't ye hear the howl o' thet dog along towards mornin'?"

Sara's eyes were fixed upon her with an interested, yet half-doubtful look. She had heard these superstitions from baby-hood, till they had become almost a part of her religion. Yet she sometimes questioned, as now.

"But, mother, mightn't these things happen, don't they happen often, and nothing come of it? I'm sure there are winding-sheets always if the tallow is poor, and that dog of John Updyke's howls every time they go away and leave him alone. It seems to me, if God is so great that even the winds and the sea obey him, he might warn us in other finer, higher ways if he wished to; besides, why should he warn us when he knows he is doing everything for our best good? You don't warn the baby when you give him medicine, even though you know he won't like taking it."

"Sairay! Sairay!" her mother lifted an admonishing finger, "be careful how you talk about the A'mighty! Babies is different from growed-up folks, and, besides, I guess ef the Lord ain't too good to count the hairs of our heads, he can even take notice of a dog's howl!" and Sara, who had the reverent soul of a little child, was once again silenced, if not convinced. Just then, too, her father entered, bringing a great gust of cold air with him as he opened the door.

"Up yet?" he asked in his big, cheery voice, as he unwound the gorgeous worsted comforter from about his throat, and shook off the sleety rain from his tarpaulin. "Waal, this fire's a purty sight, I vum, for it's a dirty night out, an' no mistake. But we'd better all turn in naow, for we must be stirrin' early to-morrer; we've got our orders, an' I'm second mate o' the Nautilus."

Fannie E. Newberry

"O father, the Nautilus? That old tub? I thought you said she wasn't sea-worthy."

"Oh, waal, not so bad as thet, quite. To be shore she's old, an' she's clumsy, but I guess she's got a good many knots o' sailin' in her yet, Sairay. I guess so. Leastwise thet's whar I'm to go, so it can't be helped, thet's sartin. Now, wife, ef you'll git out my kit," and he turned with some directions concerning his departure, while Sara, feeling she was not needed, crept silently up to bed, her soul distracted between gloomy forebodings, and the effort to trust in God and hope for the best.

The next morning, however, broke clear and fine, which was a great comfort; for whatever storms and dangers her father and friends must and would, doubtless, meet on the great ocean, it was something to have them start with fair winds and sunny skies.

All were up before dawn, except the baby, who slept on in blissful unconsciousness of any impending change; and soon the women stood, with their shawls over their heads, down on the sandy, crescent-shaped beach, watching the last preparations.

It was an impressive scene, and never lost that quality to Sara's eyes, though she had been used to it since infancy. As she stood now, near but hardly a part of the noisy throng, she was about midway in the crescent, at either end of which there gleamed whitely through the morning mist the round tower of a lighthouse.

These were only nine miles apart as the bird flies, but over thirty when one followed the concave shore; and the eastern light warned of treacherous rocks jutting out in bold headlands and rugged cliffs, while the western served to guide the mariner past quite as treacherous shallows, and a sandy bar which showed like the shining back of some sea-monster at low-tide.

Within this natural harbor was the little fleet of sloops, smacks, and schooners, getting up sail, and shipping some last half-forgotten supplies, while numerous smaller craft were paddled or rowed about, closer in shore.

The wide white beach, unbroken for a considerable sweep by even a headland, was now alive with an excited crowd - talking, laughing, weeping, and gesticulating, while back on the higher ground could be seen the small, straggling village, of but little more than one street, where nearly all the houses turned a gabled end to the highway, while a well-trodden path led through a drooping gateway to a door somewhere at the side or rear.

There were few trees to hide their unpainted homeliness; but some windows showed house-plants and muslin curtains within, while the most noticeable architectural features were the long, open sheds, used for cleaning and packing fish, and a bald, bare meeting-house, set like conscious virtue on a hill, - the only one to be seen, just back of the village, and only worthy the name because there was nothing whatever to dispute its claims in the way of highlands in that region.

As Sara stood half dreamily taking it all in, more by imagination than eyesight, for it was still mistily gray, except off to the east beyond the Cliff light, where the sky was brilliant with the first crimson blush of the morning, a man approached her, a young fellow, still tall, trig, and ship-shape in figure, as few seamen are apt to be after thirty.

"Good-morning, Sairay," he said respectfully; "we've got a fine day for the start, a'ter all." "Yes, Jasper, very fine, and I'm glad enough. The last start was dreadful! I cried all the next night, for, don't you remember? the wind kept rising till it was a perfect gale, and I couldn't help thinking of that dreadful Mare's Head Point. Mother was sure you'd get there about midnight, and saw signs and warnings in everything."

He laughed cheerily.

Fannie E. Newberry

"Oh, she enjoys it, Sairay; don't 'grudge her that comfort, for a'ter all we mostly gets home safe, barrin' a broken rib perhaps, or a finger. I've had three falls from the rigging, and one wreck, and I'm pretty lively yet!" A general movement seawards interrupted them. This was the final scene, the actual start. He held out his hand quickly.

"Well, good-by, Sairay."

"Good-by, Jasper. You'll look after father? That is, he's getting old, you know, and if anything should happen" -

"I won't forgit, Sairay. I'm on the Sea Gull, but I'll see him now and then. Good-by."

His voice was wistful, but his eyes even more so, as he clasped her hand in a quick, strong pressure which almost hurt her, then turned, and went with great strides towards his father's long-boat just about pushing off; for this was Jaspar Norris whose father was captain of the fleet, and by far the richest and most consequential man in Killamet.

Sara turned from the young man's hand-clasp to her father's embrace.

"Waal, Sairay, we're off, an' good luck goes with us, ef a man kin jedge by the weather. Good-by. God bless you, darter!"

Sara could not speak, but she held him close a minute, then stood with tearful eyes and watched him embark, telling herself he had always returned safe and sound, and surely he would again. Even her heartache could not dull the beauty of the scene, as, with all sails set, the white-winged vessels glided smoothly out toward the open sea, and suddenly her face grew bright, and she caught her breath in excitement, for just as the leader rounded the lighthouse, the tips of the masts caught the first rays of the rising sun, and gleamed almost like spear-points in the strong light, which soon inwrapped the whole fleet in a beautiful glow. Others saw it as well as herself, and some one shouted, "A good sign! A good sign!" while a hearty cheer rose from the little group of women, children, and old men upon the beach.

Sara joined in it, and felt glad as well as they; for while she might have doubts of howling dogs and dripping candles, this seemed an omen that heaven itself might deign to send as a comfort to their anxious hearts.

Fannie E. Newberry

CHAPTER II

STORM AND TROUBLE

They turned homewards presently, and Sara, walking between the now momently subdued Morton and Molly, heard her name called with a purity of pronunciation so seldom accorded it in Killamet that she knew at once who spoke.

"It's Miss Prue, children; run on home, while I stop and see what she wants," she said, turning from them and passing through the little gateway in a neat white paling fence at her side. Then she followed the path to the door, as usual near the rear of the cottage, but here prettily shaded by a neat latticed porch, over which some vines, now bare of leaves, clambered, while a little bay-window close by was all abloom with plants inside. Between the plants she caught a glimpse of a smiling face, which presently appeared at the door.

"Good-morning, Sara. Come in a minute, child. I haven't seen you this fortnight!"

Sara smiled up into the kind elderly face, around which a muslin cap was primly tied.

"No, Miss Prue, I've been very busy getting the nets and father's clothes ready; he's been expecting the start every day."

"Yes, I suppose so. What a fine morning for it! I've been watching them from the skylight through my binocle; 'twas a brave sight!"

"Yes, beautiful, only that father is getting old for such hardships. I dread his going more and more every time."

"Ah! but where will you find a stouter heart, or a steadier hand and eye, than belong to good old Reuben Olmstead? He can put many of the young men to shame, thanks to his temperate life! Your father is one of the best types of his class, Sara, - brave, honest, and true, - did you know it?"

As she spoke, she led the girl from the tiny entry, with three of its corners cut off by doors, into a pleasant room lighted by the aforesaid bay window. It had a bright red-and-green square of carpeting in the centre, with edges of fine India matting; a large cabinet of seashells and other marine curiosities occupied one end; a parrot was chained to a high perch near an open Franklin stove at the other, and the walls between were decorated with queer plates and platters of dragon-china, while great bunches of tassel-like grasses and wings of brilliant feathered fowl filled the odd spaces.

Motioning her guest to a small easy-chair, Miss Prudence Plunkett took her own, one of those straight-backed, calico-cushioned wooden rockers dear to our grandmothers, and drew it up opposite the girl's.

"No, child, you musn't worry! Reuben Olmstead's a good sailor yet, and, better than all, a good man. His Father will look after him more tenderly than you can," giving her cap an odd little jerky nod, which caused the parrot to suddenly croak out, -

"'Taint neither!" "Hush, Poll, nobody's talking to you! It's astonishing, my dear, how much that creature knows. She thinks when I nod my head I'm trying to convince her of something, and it always makes her quarrelsome."

"'Tis too!" croaked the bird again, determined to get up an

Fannie E. Newberry

argument, if only with herself.

Sara had to smile in spite of her sadness, at which the creature gave such an odd, guttural chuckle, that she laughed outright.

"That's right; pretty Poll, nice Poll! Cheer up, cheer up!" she rattled off, looking, through all these merry outbursts, so unutterably solemn, that the effect was ludicrous in the extreme.

"Silly thing!" said Sara, wiping her eyes. "She always will be heard; but while I think of it, I must tell you how I've enjoyed your 'Studies in Russia' that you lent me, Miss Prue. It must be fine to travel and see the world!"

"Yes; and it's decidedly comfortable, too, to sit by a good fire and see it through other people's eyes, Sara. These thrilling adventures, these close shaves from shipwreck, fire, frost, and robbery, are much pleasanter to read about than to realize, I imagine. Do you know, I always feel like adding a special thanksgiving for books to my daily prayer. What *would* my lonely life be without them?"

Sara's eyes kindled.

"I've felt so, too, Miss Prue; and another for you, because you have helped me to enjoy so many!"

"All right, my dear, remember me in every prayer, if you will. It's doubtless better thanks than I deserve, but I won't refuse anything so good; and now what shall it be to-day, more Russia?"

"You said something about one, - 'A Trip through Siberia,' wasn't it?"

"Oh, yes!"

The elder woman stepped across the room, and opened a glass door screened by a thick red curtain, thus displaying several book-shelves thickly packed, from which she selected the volume named; then handing it to Sara, who had risen to depart, said gently, -

"My dear, I don't like that little line between your eyes; it looks like discontent; or is it only study?"

Sara flushed.

"Something of both, perhaps."

"Smooth it out, child, smooth it out! No one can hope for wisdom until he has learned patience; now is your time to cultivate your own. Did you ever see a mountain top that could be reached without a hard scramble, Sara?"

"I never saw a mountain top at all, Miss Prue," smiling whimsically. The elder woman laughed.

"Then you have so much the more in store for you; for I'm sure you will see one some day, if it is only the Delectable Mountains above. Meanwhile, climb on, and keep looking up."

"I'll try," said Sara humbly, and took her departure, comforted and inspired, as always, by this cheery old maid, whose lover had lain over twenty years beneath the waves, never forgotten, never replaced, in the strong, true heart of his unmarried widow.

When Sara reached home she found need for her patience at once, for the baby was crying, and her mother looked cross and fretful.

"Wall," she said in her shrillest tone, as the door closed behind the girl, "you've come at last, hev you? An' another book, I'll be bound! Pity you couldn't turn into one, yourself; you'd be about as much use as now, I guess!"

"Then we'd both be 'bound,' mother, wouldn't we?" trying to speak lightly. "Give baby to me, won't you, you're tired."

She held out her arms to the screaming child, who went to her at once, growing more quiet the moment he felt her tender clasp.

"There! Now I hope I kin git a minute to myself. Where you been, anyhow, Sairay?"

"At Miss Prue's - she called me in. Mother, there's been a pin pricking him! See here, poor little fellow!" and Sara held up the bent bit of torture, then threw it into the fire, while the relieved baby smiled up at her through his tears and cooed lovingly.

"It beats all how he likes you, Sairay!" said the mother in an apologetic tone. "I never thought of a pin, an' it allus makes me ready to fly when he yells so. What did Miss Prue hev to say?" "Oh, not much; her parrot kept interrupting," laughing a little. "I always talk with her about her books or curiosities, nearly; how pretty it is there!"

"Miss Plunkett comes o' good stock. Her folks hev been sea-captings ever sence they was pirates, I guess. And she's rich too; she must hev as much as two thousand in the savings bank down to Norcross, 'sides her nice home."

"She's good!" said Sara with emphasis, as if nothing else counted for much.

"Wall, nobody's goin' to say she ain't in Killamet, Sairay, leastways, not many. In course she's ruther top-headed an' lofty, but it's in the blood. Ole Cap'n Plunkett was the same, and my! his wife, - Mis' Pettibone thet was, - she was thet high an' mighty ye couldn't come anigh her with a ten-foot pole! So it's nateral fur Miss Prue. Now, Sairay, I'm goin' over to my cousin Lizy's a while, an' if baby - why, he's gone to sleep, ain't he?"

Sara nodded smilingly, and her mollified mother said, more gently, -

"Wall, my dear, lay him in the cradle, an' then you kin hev a good time a-readin' while I'm gone. I s'pose you kain't help takin' to books arter all, seein' as your ma was a school-ma'am."

"Thank you," said Sara, more for the kindness of the tone than the words, and the little domestic squall that time passed over quite harmlessly.

But these were of daily, almost hourly occurrence. Sara's larger, broader nature tried to ignore the petty pin-pricks of her stepmother's narrower, more fretful one; but at times her whole soul rose up in rebellion, and she flashed out some fiercely sarcastic or denunciatory answer that reduced the latter to tears and moans, which in time forced from the girl concessions and apologies.

To do the little woman justice, she was often sorely tried by Sara's grand, self-contained airs, - unconscious as they were, - and by her obliviousness to many of the trivialities and practicalities of life. Mrs. Olmstead loved gossip, and Sara loathed it. The woman delighted in going to tea-drinkings, and afterward relating in detail every dish served (with its recipe), and every dress worn upon the momentous occasion; the girl could not remember a thing she had eaten an hour later, nor a single detail of any costume.

"But, Sairay," her mother would urge, after the former's visits to Miss Prue or Mrs. Norris, places to which she was seldom asked herself, except with great formality once a year perhaps; for the early and life-long friendship these families had extended to Sara's own mother was not so freely bestowed upon her successor. "But, Sairay, think! You say Mis' Jedge Peters from Weskisset was there; *kain't* you tell what she wore? Was it black silk, or green cashmere? and was the sleeves coat, or mutton-leg? and do think if she had on a cap, kain't you?"

Fannie E. Newberry

"I know she looked very nice," Sara would reply helplessly; "but, really, I can't think, mother. You see, she was telling about the work in the hospitals, - the Flower Mission, they call it, - and I was so interested I couldn't take my eyes off her face."

"Wall, then, the supper, Sairay. You must know what you was eatin', child! Did Mis' Norris use her rale chany that the cap'n brung over, or only the gold-banded? And did she hev on them queer furrin' presarves, with ginger an' spices in 'em, or only home-made?"

"Well, let me see. I think they had spices, that is, I'm not quite sure, for Captain Klister was there, and he got to 'reeling off a yarn,' as he said, about the mutiny at Benares in '57, when he was buying silks and shawls there, and I didn't notice just what was served, I was listening so intently."

At which the poor woman, greedy for news, would flare up and abuse her stepdaughter roundly, bringing up, each time, every former delinquency, till Sara either turned under the weight of them and felled her with a sarcasm, or, more wisely, fled to her attic and her books for solace.

Thus some weeks slipped by, bringing milder and more settled weather; but, as if winter and spring had roused all their forces to repulse the irresistible oncoming of the summer, along towards the beginning of May there was a cold storm of wind and sleet, lasting three days, which blasted the too confiding and premature fruit-buds, and ruthlessly cut off the heads of all the peeping, early wild-flowers.

Sara, surrounded by the children, stood looking from the window one afternoon, soon after this storm broke.

"How glad I am she didn't take baby!" she said, pressing the little fellow's cheek against her own. "I felt those last two sultry days were weather-breeders. Do you remember whether she took her heavy shawl, Molly?"

"No, I don't b'lieve she did; wait, I'll see."

The little girl, always alert as a bird, ran and peeped into the wardrobe, then called out, -

"No, here it is! I thought she didn't have it. She took her other, 'cause it's newer. She'll be awful cold to pay for it, won't she, Sara?"

"I'm afraid she'll take cold," said the older girl, with a worried look. "Put another stick on the fire, Morton, and shut the shed door tight when you come through. How the wind does blow!"

Mrs. Olmstead had gone early that afternoon, with a neighbor, to attend the funeral of a friend in the next village, and must return through this storm in an open wagon, very insufficiently clad.

It was dark before the party arrived; and as she came in shaking her wet clothes, and trying to make light of her shiverings, Sara looked at her in alarm.

"You've taken cold, mother," she said, handing the eager, crowing baby to Morton, and hurrying to divest the little woman of her wet wrappings.

"No, I guess not," she answered hoarsely, her teeth chattering so that she could scarcely speak; "but I'm ch - chilly now."

She huddled over the fire, while Sara and Molly brought warm, dry clothing, and chafed her bloodless hands. Their solicitude touched her.

"You was allus good to me, girls!" she said gratefully. "I feel lots better now. This fire's rale comfortin'!" bending almost into it in her desire for warmth.

But the vociferous baby would no longer be silenced; and she

Fannie E. Newberry

took him from Morton's arms to her own, hugging him close, and growing warmer at once from the contact of his dear little body.

"It's good to be home agin," she murmured sleepily. "I hope your pa's safe at anchor to-night: it's terrible bad weather, Sairay."

"Where did the rain overtake you, mother?" asked the latter, as she hurried about preparing a cup of hot tea and a plateful of food.

"Jest this side the cross-roads; and, my! how it did drive! We got it e'enamost in our full faces, an' it cut like a knife; but 'twas jest as fur back as 'twas forwards, an' Mis' Ruttger was as anxious to git home to her young uns as I was. Yah-h! but I'm sleepy!" with a long yawn.

"You'd better get right to bed, mother, as soon as you've eaten this; and I'll undress baby and bring him to you. You're warmer now?"

"Rale comf'able, thank ye. I do hope they ain't got any such wind out to the Banks! You ain't asked me about the funeral, Sairay."

"I was so busy, mother; were there many there?"

"E'enamost a hundred, I should think; they come from as far away as Norcross an' Weskisset. P'fessor Page of the seminary was there, an' he asked after you; he said you was a fine scholar. Then there was the Pettibones, an' the Hornblowers, an' the Scrantouns. Oh, 'twas a grand buryin'!"

"Did they all wear crape tied round their arms? and how many white horses did you see?" broke in Molly. "If you saw seven in a row, it means you'll die 'fore the year's up. I never saw but five."

"Hush, Molly! Don't talk such foolishness! Come, mother, your voice sounds very hoarse and tired. Hadn't you better get right to bed?"

"Wall, I guess so; but don't hurry me so, Sairay! I kain't a-bear to be hurried! An' I'm tryin' to think how many horses I did see, but - I've - forgotten."

Another long yawn, while her head drooped wearily; and Sara, alarmed at her white face and the purple rings about her eyes, hurried her away without more ado, in spite of her drowsy and fretful resistance. She had scarcely touched the pillow, however, when she dropped into a heavy slumber; and the girl, filled with vague forebodings over her, and also because of the storm, sent unwilling Molly up-stairs alone, and camped down, fully dressed, before the fire, with a pillow and comforter.

The next thing she realized was the feeling that she was rising out of unknown depths of nothingness; and, after one bewildered glance about the room, she finally became conscious of a faint, hoarse voice calling, "Sairay! Sairay!"

She dragged herself to her feet, all cramped and stiff from her uncomfortable position, and at last, fully aware of her surroundings, answered, "Yes, mother, I'm coming!" as she hastened to the bedside.

Bending over it, she fairly started at the pallor of the face upon the pillow, from which the dark eyes seemed starting with an expression of pain and anxiety which set her heart to beating heavily.

"Sairay," whispered that strange voice, "I'm sick - I'm awful sick - in here."

The hand, already at her side, pressed it more closely, and her brows contracted with pain.

"O mother! what is it? your lungs? You've taken a dreadful cold."

She nodded; and Sara flew to call Morton, and send him for the doctor, then heated the flannels her mother asked for, and vainly tried to soothe the now frightened and crying baby.

It seemed an age till the doctor came stamping in, - a pudgy little man, with an expression of unquenchable good-humor on his round, florid face.

"Well, well," he said briskly, rubbing his hands before the freshly kindled blaze, "caught cold, has she? Lungs sore? That's right! Plenty of hot flannels. Now, let me see."

Having warmed himself, he proceeded to examine the sick woman; and Sara saw that his face was more serious as he turned away. He gave her careful directions about the medicines, and said he should look in again after breakfast (it was now towards morning); then tied his hat down with an old worsted tippet, and prepared to depart.

Sara followed him outside of the door, unmindful of the sweeping gusts of wind, and his admonitions to stay indoors or she too would be ill.

"Yes, doctor, but just a moment; what is it?"

"Pneumonia."

"Oh! and is she very sick?"

"Well, you look after her just as I tell you, and, God willing, we'll pull her through. Now go in and dry yourself quick! I don't want two patients in one house."

He pushed her in, shut the door behind her with a bang, and was gone.

The memory of the next three days was always like a troubled dream to Sara, - one of those frightful dreams in which one is laboring to go somewhere, to do something, without success. Work as she would, day and night, assisted by the kindly neighbors and the frightened children, she could not stay the progress of that fatal disease; and on the fourth it terminated in the going out of that life which, with all its faults, had been kindly in impulse at least.

As Sara bent over her mother at the last, trying to win a word, a look, the closed lids were raised a moment, and the dying woman said feebly, "Sairay, you've - allus - been good! Don't leave - the baby. There's - the - money;" and, unable to finish, her voice ceased, her tired lids closed for their last, long sleep. She would never find fault, never give commendation, again. How the thought smote Sara as she stood helplessly gazing down upon her through her blinding tears!

"O mother, mother! I ought to have been more patient," she moaned as they led her away; "but I will try and make amends by my goodness to baby."

"Yes, that's right," said Mrs. Ruttger, wiping her eyes. "We kain't none of us help what's passed atween us an' the dead, but it oughter make us better to the livin'. Not thet I blame you, Sairay; some folks, even good ones, is dretful tryin' at times; but I know jest haow you feel, fur I've been thar myself."

There is among these honest fisherfolk a strong feeling of communism, which shows itself in the kindliest ways. They may be close-fisted, hard-headed, and sharp-tongued with each other when well and prosperous; but let poverty, wreck, illness, or death overtake one of their number, and the "nighest" of them at a bargain will open heart and purse with an astonishing generosity.

Sara found all responsibility taken out of her hands. In fact, Miss Prue, finding her standing in the midst of her room with

Fannie E. Newberry

her hand pressed to her head, gazing bewilderedly about, and asking softly, "Where am I?" took her vigorously in hand, and soon had her in bed, where, exhausted as she was, she slept for hours without dreams or movement, - a sleep which doubtless saved her an illness, and brought her strong young body into excellent condition once more.

Through all this Sara longed inexpressibly for her father, but knew it was hopeless wishing.

All she could do was to intrust the news to a fishing-smack which was about leaving harbor, and might possibly run across the Nautilus somewhere on the broad highway of the ocean. Yet, even then, he could only return in case of some lucky opportunity; for the fleet would not put back for weeks yet, as this was their harvest-time, when even the dead must wait, that the necessities of the living might be supplied.

After a few days things were strangely quiet and natural once more.

Morton and Molly, thoroughly subdued for the time by recent events, helped her about the house, the short winter's term of school having closed for the long vacation.

Even the baby seemed less fretful than before; and the lengthening, softening days went by in a quiet that left Sara many hours for her beloved books.

But the children were needing clothes, and she herself must have a cotton gown; so, as the little store of silver in the old blue teapot had been almost exhausted by the simple funeral requirements, she put on her sunbonnet one afternoon, and leaving the baby, with many injunctions, to the care of the twins, started to call on Squire Scrantoun, who had for many years been her father's banker.

The old gentleman's office was in a wing of his big yellow house of colonial architecture, and was entered by means of a glass door, which now stood open in the balmy warmth of an early June day.

Stepping within, she found him reading a paper, from which he glanced up to scowl inquiringly at her over his glasses, afterwards relaxing his brows a trifle as he observed, -

"Oh, it's you, Sara: come in, come in! Here's a seat. Now, what can I do for you?"

"Thank you, squire; I came to get some money if you please."

"Money? Oh, yes, certainly. Want to borrow a little, eh? Well, I guess I could accommodate you; how much?"

She looked up inquiringly. "Not to borrow, squire; but I've had extra expenses, as you know; and, as father always leaves his money with you" -

The squire put down his paper, and looked at her so queerly the sentence died on her lips.

"I haven't any money of your father's - don't you know? He drew it all just before he sailed, and took it home; said his wife wanted him to. She had dreamed of a good place to hide it in, I believe."

He smiled sarcastically as he made the explanation; and Sara, in her new tenderness toward the dead mother, resented this smile.

"Mother was a good manager," she said warmly, "and father always trusted her."

"Oh, of course! Reub Olmstead always trusts everybody; he's born that way. But didn't she tell you where she'd put it before she died?"

"No; but now I remember, she tried to, I'm sure. She began

Fannie E. Newberry

something about the money, but was too weak to finish - poor mother!"

"Quite likely; it's a pity she couldn't have finished. But then, you'll find it somewhere. Look in all the old stockings and sugar-bowls, - there's where these people generally stow away their savings, - and if you don't find it, why, come to me; I can let you have a little, I guess, on interest of course."

He took up his paper again; and Sara, feeling sore and resentful, rose, said a curt "Very well," and walked out.

Two years ago she might not have noticed his contemptuous reference to "these people," nor to her father's innate trust in human nature; but now, for some reason, they rankled, and she was glad to get beyond the reach of his small, keen blue eyes and rasping voice.

CHAPTER III

A SEARCH AND ITS ENDING

Sara had not walked far, however, before she began to feel the silent, irresistible influences of the day. It was the balmy blossoming time. The whole atmosphere was rich with sweet scents and sounds, while the sky had that marvellous depth and tone which makes the name of heaven seem no misnomer.

The sea, limpid and tender, wooed the shore with gentle whispers and caressings, which seemed to have no likeness to the wild rushes and blows of two months before. She looked towards it wistfully, - for Sara loved the sea, - then, yielding to the homesick impulse, turned from the narrow street to the beach, and walked briskly away towards a spur of rock which jutted into the water sharply at some distance away.

Arrived here, she sought with assured footsteps a certain zig-zag way - it could hardly be called a path - which wound in and out among the bowlders, skipping some, leaping others, trenching on the edges of little pools left in some rocky hollow by the high tide, and finally led her, after a last steep scramble, into a niche of the sea's own hollowing, which she had always claimed as her own.

Seated just within, she could look down upon a narrow cause-way, into which the water came tumbling through an aperture in the rocks much like a roughly shaped gothic window, and, having tumbled in, tumbled out again, with much curling and

Fannie E. Newberry

confusion, leaving its angry foam in sudsy heaps along the rocky edges which opposed its farther advance.

This bit of nature was named the "Devil's Causeway" by the natives, who have a way of bestowing all particularly grand and rugged sites upon that disagreeable personage; but Sara, having no mind to give up her favorite spot to his satanic majesty, always named it to herself the "Mermaid's Castle," and had a childish legend of her own about an enchanted princess confined here and guarded by the sea until the coming of the prince, - her lover.

Happy to be here once more, Sara leaned back against the rock, which felt warm, kindly, and familiar; then, removing her sun-bonnet, fanned her flushed face, and looked dreamily away to the pale opaline horizon, against which some sails showed inkily, like silhouettes.

She was wondering vaguely why sails should look so white in shore and so black far out to sea, when she was startled by a sharp tap! tap! apparently at her very elbow.

She jumped a little, then listened wonderingly. It came again - tap! tap! tap! - then a pause; and then an unmistakably human exclamation of impatience, while a bit of rock went whirling past her, to plunge with a resounding thud into the torrent below.

She leaned just the least bit forward and looked around the side of her alcove to see a funny sight. There stood a little man in the attitude of the Colossus of Rhodes, his bare bald head red and perspiring, and his eyes glaring through huge gold-bowed glasses at a bit of rock in one hand, which he had evidently just broken off with the hammer in the other.

He was muttering something unintelligible to Sara, and looked altogether quite queer and cross enough to be a denizen of this ill-named locality.

Sara, laughing to herself at the funny apparition, was drawing into the rocky shell again, when a mischievous puff of wind suddenly caught her gingham bonnet from her limp grasp, and sent it flying down the chasm after the piece of rock.

She heard the exclamation again, louder and more guttural than before, then the full moon of a face peered around her sheltering wall, and the voice said, -

"Hein! A yoong mees! Beg pardong, then - have I deesturb you?"

"No, sir," rising to her feet; "only I've lost my sunbonnet!" looking ruefully down to where it hung tantalizingly in sight, but far out of reach, on a jutting point of rock. He looked too, then shrugged his shoulders with a sympathetic air.

"If I have only been some tall now, mees, or if I could some climb down there - but, alas!"

He shook his head, and threw out his hands with a helpless motion, and just then a clear whistle rose from the base of the cliff, giving the tune of "Annie Laurie." The two looking down then caught a glimpse of a strong white hand, issuing from a black coat-sleeve, which was extended towards them, as the nervous-looking fingers grasped a ledge of rock preparatory to a spring, when the little man burst out, -

"Ha! Mine nevew! Robare, Robare, look! look dis way!"

The whistle ceased, and a head was thrust forward, - a well-cropped, chestnut head, - while a voice as clear as the whistle sang out, -

"Hello, uncle! That you, up there? How did you make it? Haven't got a rope to give me a lift, have you?"

"No, no, vait! Dat - dat - zing - Oh, you tell he!" turning impatiently to Sara, for, in trying to speak quickly, his limited

Fannie E. Newberry

English had quite deserted him.

She called out obediently, in her rich young voice, -

"Wait, please! Do you see the sunbonnet just above your head?
If you will get it and go around to the beach, I'll meet you, and
point out the way up here." "Indeed I will!" was the quick and
courteous response; and she saw the fingers tighten, then the
head give a little spring upwards, when the hand clutched the
bonnet, and all disappeared.

"I have it," was called up an instant later. "Now for the beach!"
Sara turned with a smile to the little man, who nodded kindly,
raising his head to lift the hat that was not there, then, with a
bewildered look, he whirled around two or three times and
gazed at her helplessly.

"Los'!" he murmured, with so comical a look of dismay that
Sara could scarcely keep from laughing outright. "Los'! an' it
ees tree now of dose hat that ees gone, alas!"

"Perhaps I can find it," she said encouragingly. "Why, what's
that?" suddenly catching sight of a bundle of things in a hollow
just below.

Sure enough, there was the hat, also a coat, and a round tin
box Sara was afterwards to know as a specimen-case. She
sprang lightly down, handed them up to the absent-minded
little geologist, and went on her way, meeting the nephew on
the lower ledge.

He lifted his hat politely as he saw her, and, holding out the
bonnet, said, -

"I presume this is your property?"

"Yes, thank you," she returned, flushing a little as she received
it. "You were very kind to get it for me."

"Indeed, no; it is you who are kind, rather! Did you pilot my Uncle Leon up that steep place?"

"Oh, no, sir! He found the way. See, after you get around this rough ledge it is easy till the last climb; that is quite steep. Just follow me a moment, please."

"As long as you wish" - he began gallantly, but she did not wait to hear; and, having led him to a spot whence he could see his uncle, she pointed out the further way, slightly bowed her head in adieu, and, waiting for no further parley, turned about and walked briskly homewards, remembering it was high time to return to the baby, and begin a search for that hidden money.

* * * * *

It was late afternoon of the next day, and poor Sara stood in the midst of her family and household treasures, looking the picture of despair. Around her was collected every description of bag, box, and bundle, also the baby, while Morton and Molly (the latter secretly delighted with all this excitement) were turning things upside-down and wrongside-out, with vim enough to have furnished Pinkerton's whole force.

But now they had come to a halt; for so far, though everything on the premises had apparently been emptied, no money had appeared, and the three stood confronting each other, with dismay written on their faces.

"*Can't* you think of another place, Molly?" asked Sara in desperation. "She couldn't have torn up the floor, could she?"

Molly's eyes danced.

"What if we had to take up every board! My! 'twould tear the old house all to pieces, wouldn't it? But, Sara, there isn't another place anywhere; we've been everywhere that even a mouse could get, I'm sure!"

Fannie E. Newberry

"Then it *must* be among these things, and we have overlooked it. Here, Morton, you take that pile; you this, Molly; and I'll attack these rags; though it doesn't seem possible that she could have put it in a rag-bag."

For a moment there was silence, as each delved and peered, the baby more industrious than all the rest, snatching at everything, to clap to his mouth, only to toss it aside for something else when he found it was not eatable.

"Well, Sara, say what you will, I'm sure 'tisn't in my heap," said Morton. "What shall I do with all these bits and papers, anyhow?"

"Let's see, it is nearly tea-time. Put them right into the fireplace, and light them to boil the kettle."

"All right; and O Sara! do let's have some crisp fried potatoes with our herring: this work has made me as hungry as a black bear!"

"Yes, yes, do, Sara!" cried Molly, hopping up and down. "And some molasses on our bread too; the butter's all gone."

"Well, Molly, you'll have to slice the potatoes then."

"Of course I will; where's the knife?" whirling about over the thickly strewn floor, glad of any change from what was becoming a wearisome and fruitless task.

"Molly! Molly! You're making everything fly! Do be more careful!"

"Yes'm," dropping suddenly into a ludicrous imitation of the waddle of a goose; "I'll stop flying, and paddle."

"You need a paddle!" muttered Morton, contemptuous of such antics; and he proceeded to stuff the rubbish into the chimney-place, adding a light stick or two.

Soon there was a leaping blaze under the squat black kettle, which the boy watched with satisfaction.

"There!" he said, "we won't have to look those over again. Why, what's baby got? It looks just like a wad of tobacco. Here, Neddie! Neddie! don't put that in your mouth; give it to brother, quick!"

But master baby had no idea of giving up his treasure-trove, and resisted so stoutly that a regular scramble ensued. For his dimpled fingers were shut so tightly over the wad that Morton could not at first undo them, and the baby, wrenching his hand away, crept rapidly to Sara, half crying, half laughing, then, with a sudden thought, turned when in front of the fireplace, and with a wild little giggle of mischief and rebellion tossed the thing into the very midst of the blaze.

The three were all laughing in sympathy, Sara on her knees before the rag-bag, Molly with knife and potato suspended in air, and Morton just as he had tipped over sidewise on the floor when the baby broke away, when suddenly Sara gave a quick, piercing cry.

"See! see! O Morton! Morton!" and reached out her arms in a desperate way, too paralyzed for the instant to rise.

Morton, following her wild glance, echoed the cry, for the supposed wad of tobacco, uncurling in the heat, was now plainly seen to be - a roll of greenbacks!

Morton sprang forward and made a lunge for them; Sara, regaining her wits, did the same, while Molly shrieked and whirled like a dervish, but alas! it was too late! Their scorched fingers clutched only a crumbling blackened roll, which fell to pieces in their grasp, and the day's search for that money, which meant all the difference between comfort and privation, had ended in a tiny heap of ashes, which a breath would blow away.

Fannie E. Newberry

For one long, dazed, dreadful minute Sara and Morton stood gazing at each other, the boy's blue eyes large as saucers, and Sara's brown ones turned to black by desperation; then the baby, frightened at the silence and their strange expressions, began to cry and tug at Sara's dress, demanding to be taken up.

This broke the spell. Molly gave way to an agony of crying; Morton said brokenly, "Oh, what will we do?" and Sara, stooping mechanically to lift the unconscious little cause of all this trouble, gave a long, quivering sigh, and murmured helplessly, "God only knows!"

And, indeed, the prospect was dark enough. Those greenbacks meant the savings of months, doubtless, put by bit by bit, for just this occasion, and to have them thus destroyed in one careless instant seemed too cruel!

After a little they could talk about it.

"Where could it have been?" sobbed Molly, making a dab at her eyes with the potato, but remembering in time to substitute the corner of her apron.

"I don't know," said Sara; "it was wrapped in brown paper, I think. Even if we had seen it, we would have thought it but a twisted scrap. Did either of you see Neddie when he picked it up?"

No one had, until Morton spied it on the way to his mouth, and all conjectures were useless so long as the little fellow could not explain.

Instead, Morton said more hopefully, "But, Sara, perhaps this isn't all there was. She might have hid it in two or three places."

Sara shook her head dubiously; such wisdom was more than she could hope for in the young mother.

"No, Morton, I don't believe there would be enough to divide. We must look this trouble squarely in the face."

"But, Sara," persisted the boy, "Jap Norris always says father's the most forehanded among them all, and rich for a fisherman. You know he never spends a cent for grog."

"Yes, Morton, I know. Poor father! it's too bad, when he works so hard for us!" and for the first time tears trembled on her eyelashes. Then, dashing them bravely away, "Well, what's done can't be undone. O baby, baby! if you knew the mischief your bits of hands have done!" holding them up, and spatting them gently together till he crowed with delight. "But come, Molly dear, where are those nice fried potatoes we're to have for supper? 'There's no use in crying for spilt milk,' you know."

Molly gave a last sob, then looked up with the sun breaking through her tears. "Burnt money's worse'n spilt milk, Sara; but I'll tell you what, when the coddies are all gone, I'll go lobster-catching, can't I? It's awful fun!"

There were few circumstances in life out of which Molly could not extract "fun" in some shape. Indeed, in less than five minutes she was laughing gayly, and caricaturing the whole scene just passed, from the baby's wilfulness, to Sara's shriek of dismay and rush for the burning greenbacks.

Sara, oppressed with care and forebodings as she was, could not help smiling, and the smile seemed to ease her of her burden just a trifle. "Well, we haven't come to want yet, thank God!" she thought hopefully.

Not want as they knew it, though the most of us might consider them little short of it. There were still herring, "coddies," and potatoes in store, and some groceries, while the pile of wood back of the shed was large for that village. Then, too, summer was near, when their needs would be fewer. To be sure, the new dresses must be given up, but they still had

　　　　Fannie E. Newberry

one change apiece, and there were some things of the dead mother's which could be used, for poverty does not admit of morbid sentimentality.

"Oh, we can live, surely, till father comes home," was Sara's summing-up that night, as she lay wide-awake in her bed after all the rest had long been sleeping. Then, turning over with the resolution to trust and fear not, she clasped the naughty baby (whom she had never thought of blaming) in her arms, and, with a last uplifting of her soul in prayer, dropped gently into slumber.

CHAPTER IV

UNCLE ADAM AND MORTON

The days slipped quietly away, and Sara managed, in the midst of all her duties, to read with the children at least one hour of each, and to get a little time besides for her own deeper studies.

She found she could take the old school-books which she had thought once so thoroughly learned, and dig new treasures from them; while the books from Miss Prue's, nearly all of a scientific character, were read and re-read with ever deepening interest.

But it was not the printed page alone that Sara studied. She had always been fond of long walks, and in these her keen eyes, directed everywhere, lost nothing that nature had to show her.

The shapes of the clouds, and their relation to the weather, the different phases of the sea, all the queer collection of weed and mollusk that it cast ashore, the formation and colors of the cliffs, the different shades and granulations in the sands of beach and pine grove; everything gave her active, hungering mind food for thought and speculation.

She seldom returned empty-handed from these strolls, and a rude little set of corner shelves she and her brother had managed to nail together, was rapidly filling with the oddest and prettiest of her findings. She managed, also, to interest the children in these things, and taught them a lesson some people

Fannie E. Newberry

never learn, - how to use their eyes.

Thus, living close to nature's heart, they could not be absolutely miserable, though want did press them closely.

Sara had enjoined secrecy on the children in regard to the money. She was naturally reticent, and dreaded the gossip of the little town, which made a nine-days' wonder of every small happening; and had besides that self-respecting pride which dislikes to thrust its misfortunes on a careless world. But perhaps more than all, a certain loyalty to the dead mother closed her lips. She would not have her blamed for her foolishness now she could not defend herself, poor thing! And they would manage somehow till father returned.

If worse came to worst, she could borrow of Squire Scrantoun, though she felt she could not resort to that humiliation except in case of actual necessity. So long as a potato or herring was left in store, she would wait for relief; but one thing did cause her most anxious thought, and that was how to procure milk for the little one.

As she stood one morning counting over the few pennies left in the old blue teapot, and wondering what she should do when they were gone, the door was flung open, and Morton, flushed and bright-eyed, entered and threw something at her feet.

It was a wild goose, limp and drabbled, and Sara looked up in surprise at the boy.

"You didn't shoot it, Morton?"

"No; but I killed it!" exultantly. "I've got the 'honk' so I can do it nearly as well as Uncle Adam Standish; and this morning I was down in a nice little cove, when I saw this old fellow light on the water close by. Then he paddled out and began feeding along the beach. So I 'honked' to him, and he answered, and I kept on, and he came closer. I'd first broken off this piece of rock to bring home and show you that bit of crystal in it, when I thought I'd use it, and I rose up and let fly! Well, it toppled him over, and I jumped out and caught hold of him before he could get away, and wrung his neck - and there's the goose, and here's the rock!"

He pointed triumphantly to each, while Molly executed a sort of scalp-dance about the group, snapping her fingers and smacking her lips, as she cried, "Won't we have a dinner, though? And I'm so sick of herring! You'll cook it for dinner, won't you, Sara?"

The young girl hesitated a moment, her eyes going from one eager face to the other with a deprecating glance. No one knew better than she how delightful this change of diet would be; but she quickly put aside her own desire, and said gently,

"I'm so proud of you, Morton! Molly and I can't complain with such a man to look after us, can we? But look at this. I have only a few pennies left, and I was wondering what we should do for milk for baby. Now, if we can all be unselfish, and let you sell this goose to Mrs. Norris or Miss Prue, it will buy milk for some time yet. Don't you see, dear?"

The boy's face flushed darkly, and all the brightness died out of it, while Molly's became as blank as the wall.

"It's all the baby's fault," he said bitterly. "We'd have had plenty of money but for him. Let him suffer too!"

"Morton!"

His head drooped at the grave tone, and Molly choked back something she was about to say.

"Could you really bear to see that little darling suffer, Morton? You know you couldn't! We all know he never meant to do such mischief. Look at his innocent little face this minute; could you see it grow thin and pale for lack of the food

Fannie E. Newberry

he craves?"

Morton gave one look, and melted.

"I didn't really mean it," he stammered; "only I'm awful hungry, Sara."

"My brave soldier! I know you are. But you're going to be the help and standby of us all till father comes home. I'll bake the potatoes to-day, you like them so, and you may have a wee bit of baby's milk to eat with them."

This appeal was not lost. The boy straightened up proudly. "Well, give me the goose," he said resolutely; "I'll take it to Mrs. Norris. I saw company driving up as I came by, so I guess she'd like it."

Molly made no remonstrance to this, except to draw down her round face to a doleful length, and drawl out a ridiculous wail common among the sailors, -

> "'I'm bound away to leave you -
> Good-by, my love, good-by!
> I never will deceive you
> No never, Mary Ann!'"

which she pointed by giving the stiffened foot of the defunct goose a last fond shake in farewell. So it was with laughter and good feeling, after all, that their dinner for that day was renounced.

But the little episode had given each a spirit of self-sacrifice, which was to help them through many hard times, while it had put an idea into Morton's head that he was not slow to act upon.

As soon as he had disposed of his goose to Mrs. Norris (who snapped it up eagerly, and paid him well, its opportune arrival saving her the great mortification of giving her friends a fish dinner), he sought out old Adam Standish, the acknowledged sportsman of the village.

As usual, he found the heavily bearded, long-haired, keen-eyed old man sitting on a bench before his cabin, and at the minute gazing down the long barrel of a shot-gun which he had just been cleaning. "Hello, uncle!" was Morton's greeting.

Every man is an "uncle" in Killamet, unless he is a "cap'n," or a "squire."

"Hello!" said Adam, lowering his gun. "Oh! it's you, sonny? Come up and have a seat," sweeping together the empty gun-shells, bits of rag and wadding, small tools, etc., at his side. "How's your folks?"

"All right," remembering with a sudden sense of pleasure the money for baby's milk safe in his pocket. "Been gunning lately?"

"Waal, some, a brace or two o' brants; jest hand me them pincers, Mort. Why? Want to buy?"

"No; I want to shoot."

"Hey? You! He, he!"

"I killed one this morning, Uncle Adam."

"Whar'd ye get yer gun?"

"Didn't have none."

"Hey? Little boys shouldn't tell squibs."

"I'm not squibbing; I 'honked' to it from behind some rocks, and then knocked it over with a stone."

"Ye did? Waal, purty good! purty good! Goin' to hev it fer

dinner, I s'pose?"

"N - no, I sold it to Mrs. Norris."

"Did, hey? What'd she giv ye?"

Morton told him, and the old man ruminated a while, as he industriously cleaned, primed, and loaded his gun, while Morton waited, watching a long, plume-like line of smoke along the distant horizon, which he knew was from a Portland steamer. Finally Adam set down the gun with a contented air, and observed, -

"Haow airly kin ye git up?"

"At three, if you say so."

"Waal, come along abaout four ter-morrer mornin', an' I'll take ye 'long o' me."

"But I haven't any gun, Uncle Adam."

"Don't need none! I'm a-goin' to show ye what guns Is *fer*. When you've got that idee bagged, it'll be time enough fer the weepon. I ain't no patience," he went on, putting his hands on his knees and bending forward impressively, "with these fellers what mangles their game. I s'pose it's plain that the A'mighty made wild fowl to be shot, but the man what breaks their wings and leaves 'em to crawl off an' die in misery ain't human, he ain't! Make clean work o' it, or let 'em alone, *I* say," and he began gathering up his traps in a manner that convinced Morton the conference was over.

So he said good-morning, and went whistling down the village street, the wind from off the sea tempering the downpour of the sun on white cliff and sand, and lifting the wide rim of his torn straw hat to caress his ruddy cheek.

Away out on the bay was a schooner tacking against the wind, while just rounding Rocky Point was a trim little yacht with all sail set, flying straight in for Killamet beach.

"How pretty she rides!" he thought, and wondered, boy-like, if when he was a big man he would sail his own craft, - the end and aim of every fisher-boy along the Atlantic coast.

As he dreamed, he turned and walked down over the satiny sand of the beach to the water's edge, and now could see that there were three people in the yacht, - a little round man with big spectacles at the rudder, a taller one, young and trim-looking in his tourist costume, who stood boldly out on the bowsprit, while a beautiful woman with blond hair leaned gracefully back in a steamer-chair.

With native courtesy Morton hastened to assist in securing the boat, and was rewarded by a hearty "Thank you, my boy!" from the younger man, and a brilliant smile from the lady, which covered him with blushes and confusion. The older man seemed in a brown study, and only glared at him absent-mindedly through his large glasses.

"Ah, Robare!" said the lady with an odd little accent, "I have now a thought; it may be this boy could to us tell of some public-house near by, to which we could go for this night."

All turned to Morton, who said hesitantly, -

"Yes, there is one, or at least there's Miss Zeba Osterhaus; she keeps store in her front window, and has rooms up-stairs that she doesn't use. Sometimes she takes in a painter fellow, or the goose-men."

"The what?" laughed the young man, advancing with a large portfolio, which he had taken from the yacht as soon as she was made fast.

"Why, the men that come for the wild geese - gunning, you know."

Fannie E. Newberry

"Ho, yes indeed! I'd like to be a 'goose-man' myself, for once in a way. What do you say, uncle and aunt; can you make yourselves contented with your geological and artistic prowls to-morrow, and let me off for a bit of a shoot?" Both gave a ready assent, and the speaker turned to Morton.

"And now, my boy, can you add to your favors by showing us the way to this - What's her name? - you mentioned, and telling me, as we go along, where I can get hold of a good guide and sportsman about here?"

As he spoke he attempted to slip a half-dollar into the boy's hand, but it was sharply withdrawn.

"I'll tell you all I can, sir, without pay," flushing as he spoke; for a sudden memory of the cruel needs at home made him almost regret yielding to his first impulse of pride and self-respect.

The young man flushed a little also, and slid he silver piece back into his own pocket rather quickly.

"Pardon me," he said in a graver tone than he had yet used. "I shall be very grateful for your information."

"Well, sir, there's old Uncle Adam Standish, he's the best I know," said Morton, as they led the way towards the village, followed by the others. "He can hit his bird on the wing every time, and he can 'honk' so's to fool any goose alive, and find the best blinds of anybody 'longshore."

"Really? He must be a genius!"

"Yes," - wondering what a genius might be, - "if he'll only let you go with him you'll have a good shoot."

"If he'll let me! Why shouldn't he? I expect to pay him for his trouble."

Morton laughed.

"*That* wouldn't make any difference. He doesn't seem to care much for money; all he notices is how a man handles his gun. If you hold it just to suit him, he'll go, and if you don't, he won't."

"How ridiculous! Well, do for goodness' sake tell me in what manner I must handle the gun that I may please this Criticus."

Morton bridled with indignation.

"He ain't a cuss, Uncle Adam ain't. He's a nice man, and he knows what he's about too. If you'd see some o' the fools that come down here to shoot you'd be particular too, I guess. They're a good deal more apt to hit their guide than the birds, I can tell you."

The young man laughed heartily.

"My boy, I hadn't the slightest intention of calling your relative names; that was simply a title many men would be proud to bear."

"That's all right." in a mollified tone; "but he isn't any relation to me. Everybody calls him uncle."

"Ah, I see. You make me feel wonderfully interested in this wise Adam, and only in a fright for fear I won't hold my weapon to suit him; couldn't you give me a lesson or two, now?"

Morton looked at the stranger askance; was he making fun of him? Then straightening his boyish shoulders, he said proudly, "I can tell you something better than that. *I'm* going gunning with Adam to-morrow morning at four o'clock, and perhaps I can get him to take you along too, if he likes your looks."

"Let us hope he may!" observed the other fervently. "What! is

Fannie E. Newberry

this the place we're bound for?" looking dubiously at the weather-worn cottage opposite, in whose gable end was a primitive bay-window, through which could be seen half a dozen jars of barber-pole candy hobnobbing sociably with boxes of tobacco, bags of beans, kits of salted mackerel, slabs of codfish, spools of thread, hairpins, knives and forks, and last, but by no means least, a green lobster swimming about in a large dishpan.

Morton wondered what this stranger could have expected better than this, and remarked encouragingly, -

"She's got carpets on most all her rooms, and she hooks the nicest rugs in Killamet, - all big flowers, or cats lying down, - the prettiest you ever saw!"

"Aunt Felicie, do you hear that?" flinging the question over his shoulder. "We are about to meet your rival! You paint flowers, and she, - just hear the alarming word, - she 'hooks' them! Cats, too, and dogs, did you say? Does the verb have a dishonest meaning here in Killamet, my boy?"

Morton stared back wonderingly, not understanding much except that in some way either he or Miss Zeba, or perhaps Killamet in general, was being held up to ridicule, and that it was his business to resent it.

"I don't know, sir," he answered stoutly, "what you mean: but if youwant to know whether Miss Zeba is a nice woman, I can tell you that; she's just as good as gold, sir! and I suppose if folks don't like our ways in Killamet they needn't come here, there's plenty of room outside, I guess."

The young man turned and gave him a critical look, which soon grew approving, then held out his hand. "This is the second time I've had to ask your pardon; will you make up, and be friends? I like you, and if they've got any more of your sort here, I shall like Killamet!"

Morton extended his hand readily enough, and felt it seized in a close, strong pressure which pleased him, though he could not have told why, and the young man turned again to his aunt.

"Here we are at - now, what is that name, my lad?"

"Miss Zeba Osterhaus, sir."

"Oh, yes! I believe I could remember it if I could once see it spelled, however" -

The rest of his sentence was broken off by the sharp jangle of the bell above the door, as Morton opened it; and the warning note brought Miss Zeba herself from an inner room.

Whatever of fun had been dancing in the young man's eyes suddenly died out at the sight of her. She was small, like a little child, but had the wan, drawn, yet sweet-looking face of a middle-aged woman, while between her shoulders she bore that fleshy symbol of Christian's burden, that painful affliction, that almost intolerable deformity for a woman to endure, a hump back.

Instantly the young man's hat was off, and the young man's voice grew almost tender, as he said, -

"We beg pardon for disturbing you, but is this Miss Osterhaus?"

"Yes, sir," she responded, with a quaint little old-time courtesy, directed with much precision, so as to include the three adults, beginning with the lady.

"And have you a spare room, or two; do you ever take in strangers for a few days?"

"Sometimes, sir, when they do be gentlefolk, like you," with a smiling little nod; "a lone woman can't be too keerful."

Fannie E. Newberry

The blond lady stepped forward and took up the word in her sweet foreign voice.

"Ah, it will be such a kindness, and we are most easy to bear, I hope you will find."

"Yes, as my aunt says, you will not find us hard to suit; we can put up with a few inconveniences, if necessary. Might we look at your rooms?"

These were found to be so neat and cheerful - in spite of low roofs and small windows - that a bargain was quickly consummated; and having planned with Miss Zeba for a dinner in half an hour, the young man turned to his little guide.

"Now," said he, with the fun leaping to his eyes again, "now for the ordeal! Will you conduct me to this Diogenes of a gunner, and have him tell you, without a lantern, whether I am the man he is looking for, or no?"

"Yes, we'll go," said Morton in a matter-of-fact tone; "but I don't think he's looking for you. He never goes a-nigh the post-office, because he says he hates a crowd; so even if you'd written some one that you were coming, he wouldn't know it."

"Ah, yes, I see; we will take him entirely by surprise, then; well, 'lead on Macduff!'"

"My name's Morton Olmstead, if you please, sir."

"And a good name too, laddie; I like it, and what's more I like you! You're going to make a fine man some day, did you know it?"

Morton's eyes kindled.

"I mean to, sir. Sara says I can if I will; she says the good God started me with a sound brain and a healthy body, and I ought to be able to do the rest."

"She does, eh?" opening his eyes surprisedly. "And who may this wise and epigrammatic Sara be, I'd like to know?"

Morton concluded to let the suspicious word go unchallenged. "Yes, sir, she is wise and good. She's been to school lots, and she's my oldest sister."

"Ah, indeed? That accounts for your unusually good English, I suppose. I had wondered at it here."

Morton felt this to be a compliment, so turned red and squirmed, not knowing just how to acknowledge it, and his friend, perhaps to relieve him, asked kindly, "How old is Sara?" having already decided she was nearing the thirties, at least.

"She's seventeen, sir."

"Is that all?" quickly. "Such a mere girl, and yet talks like a wise-acre, eh? How does she look?"

"Well, she's tall, and walks straight and proud-like, and her hair's kind of copper-colored where the sun shines on the waves in it, and her eyes are big and brown, and can drag a lie right out of you, sir; but when she laughs her teeth shine, and there's a dimple in one corner of her mouth, and she looks pretty well."

"H'm, I should think likely," said the young man in a musing tone, then, as Morton turned a sharp corner, "What, that way?"

"Yes, sir; there's Uncle Adam now, sitting on his bench smoking, and he looks good-natured; aren't you glad?"

CHAPTER V

MADAME AND "THE PRINCESS"

For once the old man was sitting quite still, doing nothing, unless you can call smoking a very dirty and ill-smelling pipe an occupation. He nodded to them and puffed away, saying between his whiffs, -

"How d'ye do, stranger? You agin, Mort? Set daown, both on ye; settin's jest as cheap as standin' raound here," indicating the bench on the other side of the door with a blackened thumb.

But neither cared to sit, and Morton lost no time in coming to business.

"He wants to go gunning with us in the morning, Uncle Adam, may he?"

Adam eyed the young man, who returned his gaze with frank, smiling eyes, without speaking.

"Kin ye shoot?" asked the old sportsman at last.

"A little," modestly.

"Waal, what - tame turkeys?" contemptuously.

"No: I have shot wild ones, as well as prairie-chickens, quail, and - deer."

"What! Be thet some o' your college sass, naow? I git so full o' thet every season, it makes me sick!"

"I'm not a college student, and I generally tell the truth. I've lived West for some years, and have had some good hunting at odd times; but, to be honest, I don't know anything about your bird-shooting here, and I'm hankerin' after an experience!"

The homely native word pleased the old man, and he smiled leniently.

"Waal," he said, removing the pipe to knock out the ashes and put it in his pocket (much to the other's satisfaction), "waal, I guess we kin fix it. Mort, here, an' me, we was goin' out airly in the mornin'. Ef you kin turn out in time, ye mought go with us. I've got a gun for you, but you'll hev to pay fer the powder an' shot, an' give me my share o' the birds."

"We won't quarrel about terms," laughed the other. "I'll be on hand without fail, and am much obliged."

"Oh, ye're welcome; good-day. Remember, four sharp, naow!" as they turned to go.

"You see," said the young man to the boy, as soon as they were beyond ear-shot, "he didn't put me through the manual of arms, after all. I feel almost defrauded of my just rights. Do you suppose I knocked the conceit out of him with my talk of big game?"

"I don't know," said Morton, "but I guess he took a liking to you. He's queer about that. Sometimes he won't look at these fancy fellers that come down from the city, no matter how much they offer. He says he can't abide 'em - that a fool of a loon is too good to die at their hands!"

"And he isn't far wrong, I'm thinking. Are you going that way? Then you will pass near the yacht, won't you? Have you any objections to taking a look at it, to see if it is safe? Oh, and by the way, there's a basketful of eatables stowed away under the stern-seat that we won't need now; couldn't you dispose of them in some way?"

"I think I could, sir," said Morton demurely, dropping his lids, not to show too strongly the joy in his eyes, for if he had been hungry in the morning, he was ravenous now.

"All right, then; good-by, my little friend - or, rather, *au revoir*. I'll see you in the morning," and the two separated, mutually pleased with each other.

A few minutes later Morton entered the home kitchen, joy beaming from his countenance, and a large basket hanging from his arm.

"Sara," he cried, "have you been to dinner?"

"No, we waited for you; but how late you are. It's after two."

"All the better, for here's a dinner to match the biggest kind of an appetite! See here, and here!"

He spread out with intense satisfaction sandwiches, fried chicken, cakes, doughnuts, and cheese, besides jellies and fruit, while Molly fairly howled with delight, and even Sara's eyes shone happily; for, unless you have lived for a week on salt herring and potatoes, topped off by a long fast since breakfast, you cannot understand how good those things looked to the hungry children.

"But, Morton, you didn't tell Mrs. Norris, did you?" Sara asked in a distressed tone. "I didn't want" -

"Now, don't you worry, Sara! I sold her the goose, and got my money - here it is; but this is another kind of game, and while we're eating, I'll tell you the whole story," which he at once proceeded to do, for, hungry as they were, they all fell to with scant ceremony.

The next morning the blond lady, being bereft of both escorts, started out for a stroll on her own account.

You have before this, doubtless, divined her to be the wife of that same little man Sara had met on the cliff; and we now formally introduce her as Madame Grandet, wife of Professor Leon Alphonse Grandet, of the Academie des Sciences at Paris, who was now prosecuting his geological studies in New England.

She herself was endowed with no mean artistic talent, her specialty being the painting of flowers in water colors, and, as she always sketched from nature, she had become almost as much of a botanical student as her husband was a mineralogical.

But this morning the quaintness and quiet of the village tempted her into a stroll down its long street, before she should seek the pine woods farther back, in search of hidden beauties, and one picture that she came upon held her spell bound for a moment. This was a small, poor cottage, painted only by the sun and rain, before which, on a tiny square of green, a baby was rolling about - a cunning little fellow with rings of silky light hair, while on the low doorstep sat a girl of such unusual appearance that the lady stared in undisguised admiration.

Her head was bent above a book, and the auburn shades of her luxuriant hair caught the sunlight in every wave and tendril; her eyes were cast down, but the dark lashes curled upward from the slightly flushed cheek thick and long, while the brows were as daintily perfect as if laid on with a camel's hair brush; the nose was straight and delicate; the mouth, now set with deep thought, firm and sweet, while the chin carried out this look of decision, and would have been almost too square but

Fannie E. Newberry

for the coquettish little cleft which gave it the needed touch of femininity.

Her complexion, unblemished, except for the sun-tinge which showed an out-of-doors life, was of that peculiar tint, neither blond nor brunette, which is usually found with hair of that coppery hue, and the whole artistic head but crowned a form whose grace and roundness not even her ill-fitting gown could conceal.

"One of nature's gems!" whispered the on-looker in her native tongue. "And what a cherub of a baby! I must make their acquaintance."

She took an orange from the satin bag hanging on her arm, and held it towards the little one, who had now toddled to the open gate, and was gazing shyly at her.

He looked at the tempting yellow apple, then back at sister, oblivious in the door-way, then once more at the coveted fruit, and was conquered.

As Madame Grandet stepped towards him, he did not retreat, but reached up his dimpled, dirty little hands (he had been making sand-pies) and caught the fruit she dropped into them.

Then he gave a delighted little laugh, which roused Sara, who raised her large eyes, now dreamy with far-away thoughts, but which flashed into pleasure at sight of the two.

"Pray pardon me," said madame with a gracious little nod; "I would not deesturb you, but the babee, he ees so sweet! You will let me give to him the orange?"

"Oh, certainly; thank you! It will be a great treat for him," rising and coming forward, with her book in her hand. "Won't you come in and rest a moment? The sun is warm this morning."

"Thank you, mooch; it ees indeed most warm! May I not here sit on the step of the door by yourself?"

"Oh, let me bring you a chair," running to get one. "There, this will be more comfortable," placing it just within the open door.

"That is true; t'anks! Come, mine babee, let me to you show how an orange is to eat, when one has no care for the appearance - it is nature's own way." She cut a tiny hole through the thick rind with her pearl-handled penknife, then put it to the child's lips and bade him suck out the juice, as the little bees suck honey from the lily-buds.

Sara watched her delightedly. How graceful, fair, and easy she was! What a beautiful dress she wore - perfectly simple, yet with an air of taste and style even her unaccustomed eyes could note. How delicate her features, how refined her voice, and with what a small white hand she managed the little knife!

She felt at once that here was a woman different from any she had ever seen before - perhaps the first one for whom she felt the word "lady" was no misnomer.

Her admiration showed so plainly in her honest eyes that the madame was inwardly amused, as well as pleased, yet not at all discomfited, for she had been used to admiration all her life.

"What is the book you read, my dear young lady, may I ask?" she said presently.

"It is Hugh Miller's 'Testimony of the Rocks,'" answered Sara.

"So?" It was the French lady's turn to look undisguised astonishment. "And does it for you have interest then?"

"Yes, indeed; did you ever read it? Don't you think it is wonderful how those long-buried veins of rock are made to tell us God's own plans and workings? I can never see a cliff that I

Fannie E. Newberry

don't begin to wonder how it was formed, and what secrets it may contain. I am like baby with his toys," smiling till her dimples deepened, "I want to break it in pieces and find out how it was made!"

"But that is joost like my Leon! Always he goes about with his hammer tapping, tapping, at every bit of stone. Is it then that you, too, are a geologist?"

"Oh, no, not that! I do not know enough, only sometimes I find a specimen; I have a few inside, if you would care to see them?"

"Indeed I care," rising at once; and when she stood before the well-filled shelves we have before mentioned, she cried out in astonishment, -

"But, surely, my Leon must see these. You have here some greatly rare bits. Ah, what a beautiful pink rubellite! I have not seen ever a finer. And this geode is most perfect. Did you yourself find them?"

"Yes, nearly all, except what my brother has brought me, and in this neighborhood too; I've never been more than twenty miles away in my life."

"And I do see you have them labelled and classed so neat as my Leon could do. You must indeed let me bring him to see you. He is my husband, and a - a - I forget now your English word how to say - but he eats and sleeps and dreams over dose minerals, and he would almost forget of me, the wife whom he adores, for one fine new piece of old rock with the print of a bird's toes therein!" Sara laughed with a merrier sound than she had known lately; and the lady, delighted to have pleased her, joined in.

"Oh! it is laugh we can now, my child, but some days it ees not so funny, for he does come home too often with no hat, or perhaps even his coat that is left behind; but the hammer - ah, he would never from that to part did he not have a single clothes left!"

Sara suddenly turned, her eyes dancing with merry interest.

"Wait! Was he here about a month ago? Does he wear glasses, and is he short and" -

"It is, it is! You have then seen him?"

"Yes, indeed!" and she related the meeting on the cliff, to the madame's genuine enjoyment.

She kept nodding her bright head, and finally burst out, as Sara told of the lost sunbonnet and its rescuer: -

"He vas my nevew, Robert Glendenning" (she pronounced it however Robare Glendneeng); "and is he not one handsome, fine young man?"

"I did not look at him long, but I think he is," blushing a little. "And are not you the party my brother told me of yesterday? I did not think then it was the two gentlemen I had met who were so kind to him. Morton is not any too good at description!"

"Morton, ah, yes, that ees the bright youth who did put my brave Robare to the rout! And he is thy brother, then? May I not know thy name also, my fair young mees?"

"It is Sara Olmstead, ma'am, and I am a fisherman's daughter."

"And I, my fisher-lass, am name Madame Grandet now, though my girl name it was Felicie."

"Oh, how pretty!"

"You t'ink? Do you know it mean 'happy,' 'fortunate,' and I

Fannie E. Newberry

am that, for I have few cares, and my husband does indulge every wish I can make. And your name, does it mean something good also?" "I have read somewhere that it means 'a princess,'" blushing more than before; "but that is hardly the meaning my name should have," giving a quick glance about upon her homely surroundings. "I do not know. You have the grand air, and - ah, I have it! I have it! You must be a King's daughter, a princess indeed!"

"But, madame, my father is plain Reuben Olmstead, a good and honest man, yet only a fisherman."

"But, no, my child, you do not yet comprehend. The King, it is thy Father in heaven, and thou must be one of those who call themselves the King's Daughters. It is a great society which does extend over the whole world of Christians, and each one of the members does take her pledge to do some good each day, for the help of mankind. It is 'in His name' that they do this, and their reward it is in heaven!" She spoke with great earnestness, and Sara listened breathlessly.

A princess, a daughter of the King of kings, endowed with the birthright of high thoughts and noble deeds, enrolled in the royal order of the Saviour of men! Surely here was a destiny grand and glorious enough to satisfy the highest ambition.

Her eyes darkened with the rush of thoughts that kept her silent, and finally she drew a long breath, looking up with such humility, yet kindling joy, that her words seemed but an echo of her glance.

"I will be one; teach me how!"

As she spoke, the baby who had been sitting on the doorstep contentedly sucking his orange, now broke through the rind of his yellow globe of sweets, to find nothing left but a bitter shell, and thereupon set up a wail and toddled over to Sara.

She lifted him up with tender words of comfort, applied a

dampened towel to his sticky face and hands, then brought him in her arms to the doorstep again, where she seated herself near the madame, who had resumed her chair just within.

The absence of any adults in the house suddenly struck the latter, and she asked, "Where is then the mother, Mees Sara?"

"In heaven," said the girl softly. "She died when I was little; and poor baby Ned's followed her a few weeks ago, since father went for the long fish."

"Ah, how sad! how sad! And have he not hear of this trouble?" "I do not know; not unless he got the word I sent by Captain Smalley. But, you see, his smack may not have sighted the Nautilus at all. It seems as if father would have tried hard to come, if he had heard," she added, her eyes growing misty; "we need him so!"

"Poor child, poor little one!" murmured the lady in her own language, then in English, "But what is it you speak, - the 'long fish'? Do not all your ships return each Saturday?"

"No; not now. That's the way they do at many of the fishing-villages, I have heard, but we are a long way from the Banks, and there's Mare's Head, which every vessel must round to make our harbor, so dangerous a point that our fleets used scarcely ever to get by all in safety; for when a man is hurrying home to his own fireside on a stormy Saturday night, he is not as careful as he should be. So now our boats stay out through the season, and when they have a big haul put into Gloucester or Annisquam to sell their fish, only bringing home such as they cannot find a market for. It saves many wrecks, and they make more money, but it is often hard on those left at home!"

"Yes, yes, that is true, I make no doubt! But do you live here quite alone, you and the babee?"

"Oh, no; there are my brother and sister, - the twins. Morton is the one I spoke of; he has gone gunning with Uncle Adam

Fannie E. Newberry

Standish, and the young man who must be your nephew, I'm sure; and Molly has gone on an errand."

"That Morton - it ees one fine boy! His air do say, 'Behold the American citizen in me!' is it not?"

Sara smiled and sighed.

"He is a good boy, and my mainstay now, for it is hard sometimes to manage for so many; but will you not please tell me some more about the King's Daughters, madame?"

Her new friend, nothing loath, went into further details of that marvellous organization, telling of the silver cross, which was a passport to the best society and gentlest treatment the world over; describing its growth by tens, its circles within circles, its active benevolences and astonishing influence - all that of which the world has been hearing, almost as a child listens to a fairy-tale, with wonder and delight, yet only half credulous.

She also promised to send her copies of those beautiful stories, "Ten Times One," and "In His Name," which first gave rise to the grand idea; and when she finally made her adieus, it was to leave Sara in a happy dream, filled with new hopes, desires, and resolutions, all petty cares for the time being quite forgotten!

CHAPTER VI

HAPPY DAYS

When Morton came home that night, it was with more of the air Madame Grandet had so graphically described than usual, for he bore two braces of birds, which he exultantly dropped, with a silver dollar, into Sara's lap.

"Why, what is this?" she asked, surprised at the money.

"It's mine," was the proud reply. "Mr. Glendenning gave it to me. He said I had earned it, as well as the game, for I had done all the hard work in bagging the birds; and O Sara, but he's a fine shot! Uncle Adam is that fond of him he's been trying to get him to stay all summer. He says he's a *man*, if he does wear short pants!"

Sara laughed.

"Two braces of birds, a dollar, and some new friends, how rich we are, Morton! You shall have a supper fit for a king, now, and I, one good enough for a princess!" with a meaning smile over her inner thought.

"Won't we? Make it a roast, Sara, with lots of gravy and stuffing, the way they do at Mrs. Norris's; and oh! I 'most forgot, when we came by Miss Zeba's, the pretty lady came out and said, 'Tell your sweet sister we will make her a morning call to-morrow, if she do please' - them's her very words."

Fannie E. Newberry

"'Those are,' you mean. Do try, my boy, to speak correctly, at least. I begin to think people are judged more by the way they speak than the way they dress, among intelligent people, so be careful."

"That's so, Sara, for Mr. Glendenning said I spoke good English, or, at least, that because you were so wise was why my English was correct, something like that."

"Why, what does he know of me?" astonishedly.

"Oh, nothing much, only I said you'd been to school, and so on. Sara, I believe I'll go up-stairs and lie down till supper's ready - I'm just about tuckered out!"

"Humph! Do you call *that* good English, Morton?"

"Well, it's just what I am, if it ain't fine talk," yawning loudly, and before she could correct him again, the urchin made a grimace of defiance, and fled up the stairs to his bed in the loft.

The announcement of that supper "fit for a king" brought him down good as new in an hour's time, and I think few royal personages ever enjoyed a meal more, for "hunger is the best sauce" now as ever.

The next morning the three from Miss Zeba's arrived, quite curious over this orphaned family the madame had talked so much about.

As for young Mr. Glendenning, ever since Morton's description of his sister, which instantly recalled to his memory a blushing, beautiful face, and a hand outstretched for the gingham bonnet in his own, he had been secretly wondering in what way he could make his surmises certainties, without ungentlemanly intrusion; so you may be sure he had no better business in hand when his aunt proposed the call, while her husband would go miles any day to view a really fine specimen.

Molly, in the doorway, painfully enchained just then to her stocking-darning, first sighted the trio, and announced in an excited whisper: -

"They're coming, Sara, they're coming! Have you got the baby washed, and the braided rug over the broken board in the floor?"

Both these important ceremonies having been attended to, she seated herself once more, with an attempt at composure, though every line of her speaking face was alert with anticipation.

"Ah!" said the madame, eying her from the road, "that must be the girl-twin, - Molly they do call her. What a *chic* little face it is! Do look with what an air she will make as if she does not see us; it ees inimiteeble!"

They turned into the little gate, much amused, and she finally looked up, with such an assumption of astonishment they could scarcely keep from laughing outright; then sprang to her feet, and made a twinkling little bow, which set the young man's eyes to dancing, and entirely captivated madame, at which Sara appeared in the doorway, with her fine Greek head, and rare smile, to give them greeting. Then Morton turned from the fish-lines he was straightening, and looked his honest, quiet pleasure, as different in manner from his twin-sister as a staid, slow proud-stepping heron is different from a flitting, fluttering, flame-winged oriole.

After madame's introductions, which were hardly necessary, as both gentlemen at once recognized Sara (the younger one with an acceleration of his heart-beats which rather surprised himself), the professor became at once immersed in the mineralogical specimens, with Sara to answer his questions.

His nephew plunged into an animated talk with Morton about blue-fishing, and the blond lady divided her attentions between Molly and the baby, whose merry little outbursts soon

Fannie E. Newberry

won the two would-be fishermen from their discussion. Molly was just then giving an account of her school-teacher, talking like a little steam-engine, all dimples, gestures, and tossing curls.

"Why, he isn't anywhere near as good as Sara in books, and you can tangle him up just like a salmon-line!" she cried. "It's lots of fun to see him when we all get to asking questions faster'n he can think; but then, he's awful good about the claws!"

"The what?" asked Glendenning. "Why, you see, when we girls catch a lobster we always keep the claws in our desk, to pass around and suck with our bread at lunch (don't you like lobster-claws? They're splendid!), and he don't mind if we sometimes take 'em out in school-hours. He says fish is good to make more brains, which we need, and when our mouths are full we can't be buzzing! We never had one so nice about that before."

"How wise this modern Aristotle must be!" the young man broke in amid the laughter. "But I doubt if even a lobster-claw could keep you still!"

The little maid gave him a shy glance, containing more of coquetry than her sister would ever know.

"I'm pretty still in church," she said, "that is, if 'tisn't *too* long. Do you think it's very bad to just look 'round at the clock sometimes? Our church clock's right under the gallery scats, behind us, and it goes the slowest of any I ever saw! Sometimes, when I've waited 'most an hour before I looked 'round, it won't be five minutes by that clock! Miss Prue Plunkett's my Sunday-school teacher; and one Sunday when I had a cold, and my neck was so stiff I couldn't move, she said it didn't better those old Jews any to be a stiff-necked race, but it certainly did me. Sometimes Miss Prue talks so't I can't understand just what she means; but Sara likes her first-rate, and so do I too, most generally."

"Molly!" came admonishingly from the corner where the shelves were, "I'm afraid you're talking too much." "Yes, she is, Sara," put in Morton earnestly. "She's just *rattling!*"

The madame leaned back, laughing in keenest enjoyment.

"I had forgotten how delightful it is that children may be in a state of nature," she said. "Ah, Robare, how can we go back to those doll-childs at the hotel, with their so fine costumes, and so of-this-world-weary airs, now? You have no doll-houses, my infants, no fine toys that move by the machine-work within, no bicycles, no anything for play; what, then, does amuse you all the day's length in this most sleepy town?"

The children stared at her with round, puzzled eyes.

What did they find to amuse them? With the cliffs, and the sand, and sea, and the nice little lobster and clam basins they knew about; and the countless shells for dishes, and fish-scales for jewellery, and kelp for carpets, and dulse and feathery sea-fern for decorations.

"Dear me!" cried Molly, "there's things enough; all we want is *time*. Here I've wasted a whole morning darning stockings and talking to you!"

The outburst that followed this *naive* confession brought uneasy Sara to her sister's side; and with a hand on one of those restless, twitching little shoulders, she managed to keep her respectably quiet through the rest of the call.

As the guests went down the village street it was funny to hear their comments.

"It ees a most fine collection, all varieties and classified most orderly," observed the professor, intent on the minerals.

"Such specimens! And impossible to keep in order!" broke out the young man, meaning something entirely different. "But

Fannie E. Newberry

the oldest is a rare one, and" -

"Ze oldest? Yes, but there be some vich are mos' rare of dose later ones, too. But" -

"The little feather head!" laughed madame out of her thought, oblivious of what had gone before, "but *jolie* and bright" -

"Zat so bright on, it ees no feddar-head, Felicie; you mistake. That was the rusty, dull" -

"Rusty! Dull! That so brilliant bird of a child! what mean you, Leon?"

"Child? Who say child?" dazedly.

"Oh, stop, stop!" interposed their nephew, raising both hands, "don't have a family jar over nothing. Uncle's on geology, and auntie on babies; don't you see?" and the discussion ended good-naturedly in a laugh all around.

They came every day after that, during their lengthened stay of a week, and often the professor would press Sara into service to direct him in his search for treasures, while madame stayed with Molly and baby; and Morton took many a delightful sail in the yacht with Mr. Glendenning after bluefish or salmon.

Those were happy, plentiful days in the little cottage, for fresh fish or game was almost constantly on their table, while the overplus, sold to their richer friends, kept baby in milk, and all in necessary supplies.

Besides, madame's quick eyes soon penetrated into the real poverty behind the hospitable, self-respecting air of the little household, and she managed in many delicate ways to assist them.

Feeling instinctively that there must be no hint of remuneration to Sara for her really valuable services as guide to her husband, she struck up a trade in wild-flowers, delicate algae, and shells with Molly, buying all that the child could bring her (and the little girl was famous for these findings), afterwards teaching her to mount them in exquisite designs on Bristol-board for possible future customers.

Morton, too, was paid a liberal percentage on fishing-tackle, etc., so that among them all the wolf was kept decidedly at bay, and Sara felt every night like adding a special thanksgiving to her prayers, because she was not forced to ask a loan of Squire Scrantoun.

CHAPTER VII

A TEA-PARTY

Meanwhile, she was learning to systemize her time so as to make the most of it, and, given a fresh impetus in her studies by this new companionship, spent the days so busily she scarcely had time, till night laid her on her pillow, to wonder where father might be, and when he would return.

So far, with the exception of the storm which had proven so fatal to her mother, the season had been quite free from gales, or "breezes" as the fishermen call them; for with these hardy people a good-sized tornado is only a "stiffish breeze" usually.

But when these new, delightful friends went away, it seemed as if everything changed. Dull, foggy days, with fitful gusts, succeeded to the lovely month just gone, and the skies were leaden and threatening.

Then, too, little by little, the wolf began creeping towards their door, for Sara, in the large liberality of her nature, did not well know how to deny the eager wants of the children, so long as she had any means to gratify them; and was not so wise in hoarding against a rainy day as an older head might have been.

Still further, to add to her gloom, baby had a slight attack of measles, over which she worried more than was necessary; and, altogether, August was for her a blue month, with only two bright spots to recall.

One of these was when Morton, red and exultant, came lugging home a mammoth express package, with Molly, fish-knife in hand, dancing about him like some crazy Apache squaw about a war-captive, though she was only impatient to cut the cord.

When her wish was finally gratified, Sara's delighted eyes beheld two volumes she had long been wishing for, and a pretty dress-pattern; Morton's caught sight of some tackle that fairly electrified him, with a suit of clothes better than he had ever owned before; Molly's darted with lightning speed to a neat jacket and hat, also a handsome herbarium book for her algae; while baby set up a squeal of joy at sight of some novel toys and picture-books, leaving Sara to the full appreciation of a dainty infant outfit below.

Of course these most acceptable gifts were from the Grandet party, - now in Boston, - who had proven themselves thus more constant than most "summer friends," and generous almost beyond belief, as Sara thought.

The other red-letter day was one when the whole family was invited to tea at Miss Prue's. They went early, as was the fashion in Killamet, Morton stiff and conscious in his new suit, and baby filled with undisguised admiration for his own new shoes, while both girls looked so unusually "dressed-up" in their Boston finery, that Miss Prue naturally concluded good Reuben Olmstead must have left his family well provided for during his absence, and had not the slightest idea how closely pressed they were for actual money.

They had been seated but a few moments, Morton gravely staring at the dragon-china with meekly folded hands, Molly tilted on the edge of her chair like a bird about to fly, and the baby on Sara's lap wide-eyed and inquiring, when Polly thought the quiet was growing oppressive, and broke out, -

"Pretty Poll! Pretty Poll! How d'ye do? Oh, you fools!" At which Molly ran over in a rippling little giggle, so infectious

Fannie E. Newberry

that every one had to join in.

Miss Prue turned to her with an indulgent smile.

"Bless her heart! It would be dull here if 'tweren't for Polly, wouldn't it? Let's see, I've a new game somewhere, from Boston; it's bits of rhyme and scraps of knowledge, I believe; I never played it, but perhaps you and Morton can make it out," and soon the two were seated, bending over a light stand, quite happy for the nonce.

Meanwhile, baby was so impressed with the dignity and solemnity of the occasion that he kept his round eyes fixed unwinkingly upon the parrot (who occasionally addressed a remark to him), until the weary lids closed, and he dropped his sleepy little head over against Sara's shoulder.

Then she and Miss Prue had a long, delightsome talk, in which she told her good friend all about the Grandet party, the order of the King's Daughters, those beautiful, impressive books of Hale's, and something - not a great deal, for Sara was naturally reticent of her inner life - of the hopes and longings kindled by them in her soul.

As the kind old maid watched her noble, expressive face, and noted the clinging little figure in her arms, she sighed, wondering, -

"Is here to be another life-long sacrifice? Are these sparkling, youthful hopes to settle down into the dull, smouldering fires of duty - a fire which will always boil the domestic kettle, and warm the family hearth, but never be a beacon-light on the hill of effort, to help the world onward?" Then she checked herself. "Is any life well lived, however humble, quite lost to the world? And does not God know better than I where to put her?" and thus ending her reflections, she turned with a brighter look to say,

"My dear, don't let *anything* discourage you from carrying out your views! I believe this life of ours is like a flight of steps leading to a throne. When we have performed all that is required of us on the first step, we must go on and up But sometimes, alas! we will not do what we should, and have to be ordered back. Then how painfully slow seems the climb to our former position! But, if we can only always hear that 'Come up higher,' and keep steadily on, slowly it may be, so slowly the steps seem but an inch high, we will surely reach the throne in time - or in eternity."

Sara's luminous eyes rested intently on her face.

"The steps may not all be beautiful or easy," she breathed.

"No, nor will be, my dear. There is a little book of essays I have, and one is called 'The Gospel of Drudgery;' I want you to read it."

Miss Plunkett rose and stepped to the book-case on the opposite side of the room, being enjoined, sleepily, by Mistress Polly meanwhile, to "Come again, and don't be long!" When old Hester appeared in the doorway, to bob a courtesy, and announce, -

"Tea is served, Miss Prue."

Hester was a character in Killamet, and must be described.

She was a pure-blooded African of Guinea, who, when a wee child, was rescued from a slave-trader by Captain Plunkett, Miss Prue's father.

The poor little black baby's mother had died during the cruel march to the coast, and the little creature, become almost a skeleton, and looking more like a baby chimpanzee than anything human, was made a pet of by the crew on the homeward voyage, growing fat and saucy daily, so that when the captain presented her to his daughter, then an infant of two years, she was as cunning a specimen of a negro baby as

Fannie E. Newberry

one often sees.

Instantly the fair little Prudence took a great fancy to her, thinking her, doubtless, some new queer kind of doll; and from that time the two were almost inseparable companions.

The little stranger was soon given free papers, formally adopted, and baptized under the Christian name of Hester Plunkett; and from her twenty-first birthday had always received wages for her services.

Her love for the family, especially Miss Prue, almost the only survivor of this especial branch, was simply unbounded; and nothing could have tempted her to leave the latter.

Even as she made the simple announcement, her great, soft black eyes rested lovingly on her friend and mistress, then turned, with a smiling welcome, upon the children.

"I'll tend the baby ef he wakes, Miss Sairay; let me lay him down now," she said, lifting him with her powerful black hands; "he likes his old Aunt Hester!" and she nestled him against her broad bosom, and bent her stately white-turbaned head caressingly over him.

Molly, who was always fascinated by her, watched every movement, her eyes dancing, and her checks dimpling with some inner thought.

"Come, what are you sparkling over now?" cried Miss Prue, taking the child's hand to lead her to the dining-room. "I know you've an idea in that little brain of yours, because it's almost ready to jump out of your eye-windows!" Molly gave a little hop - she seldom walked - and caught the aged hand in both of hers. "I'll tell you, Miss Plunkett, but you musn't tell anybody, will you?"

"I'll try to keep it a secret, Molly."

"Well, what do you s'pose Hester looks like?"

"Now, Molly! You wouldn't make fun of good old Hester, would you?"

"But I'm not making fun, Miss Prue, indeed and indeedy I'm not, only she *does!*"

"Well, like what, Molly?"

By this time they had reached the dining-room, and Molly drew her behind its door, to whisper mysteriously, -

"She looks just like Rocky Point when there's a high wind. Then the rock stands up there black and big and square, just as Hester does; and her muslin turban is the spray up over the top of it, don't you see?"

Miss Prue nodded comprehensively, for the resemblance of the tall, straight negress to that bold headland was something she could recognize herself, now it was brought to her notice.

"I think you're right, dear; but come, our supper is waiting. Pray excuse me, Sara, for keeping you and Morton standing here; this little lady-bird and I have been exchanging confidences behind the door!"

What a supper it was! Well worth waiting for, Morton thought, for the queer foreign-spiced preserves and the hot pickles (which made Molly wink tearful eyes rapidly, and say, "No more, thank you, ma'am!" with great promptness) were all there; besides dainty cakes, such as only Hester could make, and tea that was to the common beverage as nectar to vinegar.

Once Molly paused, inspecting a small cream-cake in her hand with a grave air.

"What is it, dear? What are you thinking?" asked Miss Prue, to whom the child was always a whole page of fun and epigram.

"I was thinking, ma'am, how does this froth get inside the cake?"

"Molly, Molly! You are too curious," said her sister.

But now an idea suddenly struck the child, rippling and dimpling over her bright face like a breeze over a little lake.

"Oh, I know!" she cried, "I know! You just churn the cream, and then pour the dough around it, of course!" which lucid explanation seemed perfectly satisfactory to herself at any rate.

All the stiffness of that first half-hour was now gone, and the rest of the stay was one riotous frolic, in which baby Ned, sweetened by a long nap and a good supper in Sara's arms, joined merrily; and, as Miss Prue watched the little party leave her gate in the late dusk, it was through misty eyes, for she could not help thinking of the home she might have known, had not the sea claimed her husband for its own.

After this happy day came a few that were anxious enough to poor Sara; for the little hoard was getting fearfully low, and now, too, the provisions were nearly gone.

"I'm afraid, Morton," she said one morning, "if we don't hear something from father this week, I'll have to borrow of Squire Scrantoun."

Molly's nose went up.

"I don't like him; he's a scowly man! Let's borrow of Uncle Adam or Miss Prue."

"But old Adam Standish is nearly as poor as we, Molly."

"No, he ain't," with a toss of her head; "he's got a heap of money! He keeps it in an old shot-bag, and I've seen it myself; he's got - well, as much as five dollars, I do believe!"

As this magnificent sum did not impress Sara so much as it should, the child concluded to drop finances for a while and attend to baby, who was busily engaged just then in pulling straws out of the broom, a loss the well-used article could ill afford.

Sara stepped past the two at their frolic and looked out of the open door.

It was a glorious morning, the air washed clean by a thunder-storm during the night, and the sea still white-capped from its violence.

As she was watching with admiration its turbulent beauty, Morton, who had come to her side, burst out, -

"Why, Sara, look in the offing, isn't that the Seagull at anchor? Why, it is, it must be! Then Jap Norris is here, and can tell us about father!"

"Are you sure, Morton? I can't make her out from here.'

"Well, I can! I know the old Sea-gull like a book; and look! look, Sara, if that isn't Jap this minute coming down the street!"

Sara looked, recognizing the straight young figure at once, and turned back to her brother with a quick pang of foreboding that slightly paled her sweet face.

"Morton," she said huskily, "he brings us news of father!"

CHAPTER VIII

NEWS FROM THE NAUTILUS

When the fleet to which the Nautilus belonged reached the Banks, everything seemed exceptionally propitious. The weather was fine and tranquil for March, and the fish fairly asking to be taken. In fact, it was all "too lucky," as old Captain Sennett of the Nautilus growled occasionally, he being, like all sailors, superstitious to the core, and "fond of his blow," as the crew put it.

They made a "big haul," with which they put into port, and after disposing of it started out again, only to make a trip as disastrous as the former had been fortunate. There was a week of the "dirtiest" kind of weather, - head-winds, fogs, and treacherous "breezes," which strained every timber in the old tub of a Nautilus, as she rolled clumsily about in the turbulent waves.

At length there came a night (it was one of those in which Sara had watched with baby during the measles) when the sea, as if scorning all previous performances, seemed lashing itself into a very climax of rage. Smutty rags of clouds flew across the ominous horizon, and spiteful gusts, apparently from every direction of the compass, caught the old Nautilus in wild arms, and tossed her about like a foot-ball.

She had sprung a slight leak also, nothing dangerous in a stanch vessel, but an added straw, which might prove the last in this straining wrestle with wind and sea, and she did not answer her rudder as her steersman could have wished.

"Will she stan' it, cap'n, think ee?" asked Reuben anxiously, as a momentary pause in the pounding and smashing found them together.

"God A'mighty knows!" was the solemn answer. "If her rudder" -

The rest was drowned in a new shriek of the blast, and Reuben threw himself flat and clung for dear life to the winch, as a wave washed over the deck, smashing everything breakable into kindling-wood, and almost drowning the two, whom instinct and long practice helped to cling, in spite of the fact that the very breath was beaten out of their bodies.

But this, bad as it seemed, was only the beginning of troubles. There were hours of just such experiences; and Reuben's strength, robust as it was, began to fail him beneath the strain.

In such storms there is no rest for the sailor. Something is needed of him every moment, especially upon these fishing smacks and schooners, which carry such small crews; and often forty or more hours will pass with literally no rest at all.

They labored on until evening set in once more, and all hands had just been ordered aft to secure a broken spar, when Nick the boy uttered a fearful cry, which gave every man a start. They followed the direction of his horrified gaze, and saw a danger which paralyzed the stoutest nerve. Just ahead was a "gray-back," - sailor parlance for a wave which is to all other waves as a mountain to a hillock, - and Reuben felt their doom was sealed, for the old Nautilus, disabled as she was already, could never stand that terrific onslaught.

With one short, desperate prayer he closed his eyes and clung with the grip of the dying to the shattered spar.

Fannie E. Newberry

It was all over in a moment. A roar like a thousand thunders, a stunning blow impossible to imagine, and then - a broad, wreck-strewn expanse, amid which those few poor atoms of humanity showed but as black dots for a moment, soon to be sucked beneath the seething waves.

By dawn of the next day the storm was over, for that gray-back had been one of those climaxes in which nature seems to delight; and, having done its worst, the winds hushed their fury, and wailed away into a chill, sullen, but clearing morning.

The remainder of the fleet, scattered in every direction by the storm, did not discover the absence of the Nautilus till mid-forenoon, when bits of wreckage, into which they sailed, soon told the pitiful story. Towards noon two bodies were found, that of the captain and steersman, afloat in the pilot-house, but no more; the fate of Reuben, the boy, and the three other hands could only be conjectured.

The next day the drowned men were given honorable burial; and many of the remaining vessels, having been almost disabled by the fury of the elements, had to make for the nearest port for repairs.

Then came a fair and "lucky" run, in which not a hand could be spared to carry the news home, for these fishermen learn to look almost with contempt upon death and disaster. Many a poor fellow with a broken limb must go days, even weeks, before he can reach a physician; and the friends on shore are left as long in ignorance of their fate.

Nearly a month had passed, then, since that awful night, when Jasper Norris, dreading his task as he had never dreaded any physical danger in his life, walked down the village street toward Sara and Morton in the cottage doorway.

The former watched him with a growing feeling of suffocation and tightness about her throat and heart, for the droop of his figure was ominous.

Had there been good news he would have given a sailors' hurrah at sight of them, and bounded on, waving his cap in welcome. But, still in dead silence, he turned into the little broken gate, and walked up the path to the door.

Sara, quite white now, and leaning for support against the jamb, kept her piercing eyes on his face, though his would not meet their gaze; while Morton rolled great frightened orbs from one to the other, as from within came unconscious Molly's gleeful babble, and the baby's sweet little trills of laughter.

"Jasper!" gasped Sara in desperation, "why - why don't you speak?"

He looked up, and made a hopeless gesture with his hands.

"Don't, Sairay," he said huskily, "don't give way, but - but I've bad news."

A great trembling now shook her limbs, and she lifted her hands as if to ward off a blow, but her agonized eyes seemed dragging the words out of him.

"Your father, Sairay, he's - he's - the Nautilus went to pieces, like the tub she wor, and he's" -

"*Drowned!*" screamed Morton, putting his hands to his ears.

"Who's drowned?" cried Molly, running to them. "Why, Jap, that you? Where's pa?"

Sara, who had not spoken, at this dropped to the doorstep, and, doubling up in a forlorn little heap, buried her face in her hands. Morton burst out crying; and Molly, with a puzzled look around, joined in promptly, thinking it the proper thing to do, though she had not yet an idea of what had really happened.

But why prolong the heart-rending scene, as little by little Jasper stammered out all the story he had to tell, and the poor children began to realize how doubly orphaned they were? This was a grief before which the loss of their. stepmother seemed as nothing. They had loved their big, kind, good-natured father as a companion, far more than a parent; and the thought of never meeting him again, of never hearing his well-known greeting after his absences, -

"Waal, waal, younkers, come and kiss your old dad! Did you miss him much, eh?" - seemed intolerable.

Sara, under this new blow, for a time lost all self-control, and broke into such a passion of grief, that Jasper, much frightened, ran for the nearest neighbor, Mrs. Updyke.

She soon appeared, - a gaunt woman, with a wrinkled visage, and a constant sniff.

"Land sakes!" she cried, upon hearing Jasper's ill news, "Yeouw don't say! Well, well, it's a disposition o' Providence, to be sure!" by which she doubtless meant a dispensation, though it did not much matter, for no one paid the slightest attention to her moral axioms just then.

By this time the news had spread, and the neighbors were flocking to the afflicted cottages; for all the drowned men had lived in Killamet, and were well known, while each had left a wife, mother, or some weeping female relative, to mourn his loss.

But all agreed that the Olmstead case was hardest, or, if they did not, Mrs. Updyke took pains to impress that idea upon them with a decisive sniff; for, being a next-door neighbor, she naturally desired that the affliction close by should outrank all other distress in the village.

But, finding Sara oblivious just now to everything but her grief, she left her to pace back and forth, wringing her hands and moaning like some caged creature, contenting herself with telling the children "they could mourn for their poor pa jest as well with less noise," while she prepared to receive the sympathetic callers with an intense satisfaction, which the solemnity of the occasion could not quench.

"Yes, it's a awful visitation," she sniffed, as the curious, friendly women flocked in; "I don't know's I ever hearn tell of a harrowin'er! Four orphans, with no pa nor ma!" (Sniff, sniff.) "Molly, when that babby squirms so, is it pins or worms?"

"He wants Sara," sobbed the poor child, whose laughter and dimples were now all drowned in tears.

But Sara, unheeding of everybody, still kept up that wild walk back and forth, back and forth, every groan seeming wrenched from her very soul; and poor baby had to squirm, - and stand it.

Ah! that is a lesson that comes almost with our first breath!

"Poor child!" said one little dumpling of a woman. "Let me take him home: he'll be amused with my Johnnie, I know. Come baby!" and, managing at length to coax him away, she took him to more cheerful surroundings, where he was soon quite as happy sucking a peppermint lozenge, and watching Johnnie with his toys, as if no father lay buried under the cruel, restless sea.

Meanwhile, awed by Sara's intense grief, the women stood about, quite powerless, and gazed at her.

"Cain't we do nothin'?" asked Betty Pulcher, who could never endure inaction. "What is there to *do*?" "Nothin'," sniffed Mrs. Updyke solemnly, "least-wise, not now. Ye see, thar won't be no funeral to make ready fur, an' the sermon won't be till a Sunday. I've gin the house a hasty tech to red it up; an' ef the

Armatts an' the Simcotes (them o' his fust wife's kin, an' his own, ye know) should come over from Norcross, we'll hev to divide 'em up. I kin sleep two on 'em, an' eat four, I guess, ef the rest on ye'll do as much."

Each one agreed to do their best, this cannibal-sounding proposition meaning nothing worse than true fishwives' hospitality; and the group had gathered in a knot to discuss in low tones the children's "prospec's" for the future, when Mrs. Norris and Miss Plunkett came in.

They were cousins, and something alike in face and manner, though the spirituality in Miss Prue's visage became a sort of shrewd good-humor in that of Mrs. Norris; and now each proceeded in a characteristic way to her duty.

Miss Prue went straight to Sara, and took the poor, unstrung little bundle of nerves into her arms, her very touch, both firm and gentle, bringing comfort to the half-crazed girl. She did not say much of anything, only kissed her and wept with her; but soon the violence of Sara's grief was subdued, and her heart-rending moans sank into long, sobbing breaths.

Mrs. Norris, after one pitying look, turned to the women.

"Don't you think, friends, it is possible that seeing so many makes her worse? We all want to do something, I know. Mrs. Deering, you're so good with children, why not take the twins home with you for to-day? Perhaps your own bairnies will help to comfort them! And, Betty Pulcher, their clothes will need some fixing, no doubt, for Sunday. You're just the one to manage that; and get Mandy Marsh and Zeba Osterhaus to help you: they'll be glad to, I know. And you, Mrs. Updyke, and Mrs. Shooter, - were you going to look after the cooking, and so on? There'll likely be a crowd over for the sermon."

As each one was given just the work she preferred, and as there seemed little more chance of excitement here, they soon separated, not realizing they had been sent home, however;

and a blissful quiet reigned.

When Mrs. Norris stepped outside to close the gate after the last one, a voice arrested her.

"Mother! mother!"

She turned.

"Why, Jap, what are you doing there?" as her son came around one of the rear corners of the little building.

"I'm just - waiting. Say, mother," tremulously, "will it - kill her?"

"Kill her? Who, Sairay? No, indeed. She's lots better now. Gracious! You look sick yourself, child!"

"I'll never do such a thing again, mother, - never! I felt as if I'd stabbed her to the heart. Do - do you s'pose it'll make her - turn agin me?"

"Gracious! No; what an idee! Why, you've worked yourself into a regular chill, I declare. Go home, and tell Hannah to fix you up a good stiff dose of Jamaica ginger right away. Well, I never!"

"Then you think she's coming out of it all right?"

"I think she's enough sight better'n you'll be, if you don't go and do what I tell you this minute; now hustle!" and Jasper, knowing his mother's decisive ways, walked away without more ado.

But not home; not to Hannah's ministering care and the Jamaica ginger, but to a little cove by the sea where, with his body thrown flat on the rocks, and his face buried in his hands, he wept like a child himself, for pure sympathy with that orphaned girl who was so dear to him.

　　　　　Fannie E. Newberry

CHAPTER IX

REBELLION

But the poor, perhaps fortunately, have little time for mourning. As the first hint of the long winter came in on the September's equinox, poor Sara had to rouse herself, and she began to look about her with despairing eyes. Friends, so far, had been most kind, and the little family had never actually suffered; but now that the few summer resources for picking up an occasional dollar were ended, what had they to look forward to in the long months to come?

Reuben Olmstead had owned the poor little cottage in which they lived, so a roof over their heads might be counted on, but not much besides; for his share in the last fishing-expedition, promptly paid over by Jasper, had soon been swallowed up by the family's needs, so greatly reduced had they become before it arrived.

Sara was not, perhaps, a good financier, - few girls of barely eighteen are, - but she had done her best, and her feeling had often been that of a mother-bird, wearied by a long day's search for worms, who always finds the mouths stretched wide as ever, clamoring for more. The task of filling those mouths seemed a hopeless one.

"What can I do?" she thought, as she sat huddled over the tiny fire one day, waiting for the children to come home from school. "The flour is all gone, and the potatoes nearly, and so little wood!"

She shivered, then turned to see if the sleeping baby were well covered, and resumed her dreary musing.

"I don't wonder our people almost welcome a wreck when they are so poor. Of course it's wicked; but if there must be storms, and ships have got to go to pieces - God forgive me! I believe I was almost wishing for one, myself! If there were only something I could do; but what can I? Here are the children; they must be cared for, and the baby above all, - what can one do when there's a baby to look after? I suppose some would say, ask her people to take him; but who is there? Her mother is dead, and her father a deaf old man who can't live long; she had no sisters, and her brothers are sailors who are off all the time. There's only her cousin 'Liza, and I couldn't give the poor little fellow up to that hard, coarse woman; besides, I promised her and I promised father to care for him myself. If I could go out into the world, it seems as if I might find a place; I am strong and young, and not afraid to work, but here there is no opportunity."

Then, after a long, silent gaze into the fire, -

"God certainly knows all about it; he could help me if he would; I wonder why he doesn't? Does he treat us as I sometimes do baby - corner us all up till there's only one way to go, and so make us walk straight? But to walk straight now looks as if it led to starvation."

Her head drooped lower, and her thoughts grew too roving and uncontrolled for connected expression; in fact, her brooding had become almost actual dreaming, when the door swung back with a bang, and the two children rushed in, Molly screaming with laughter and resistance as she fled before Morton, who was close at her heels.

"Sara! Sara! make him stop! I" -

Fannie E. Newberry

She was stopped herself by a sudden crash, and all three stood in blank affright and astonishment as the oval, gilt-framed mirror, which hung between the front windows, fell to the floor in the midst of them, and shivered into a dozen pieces. It had been one of the proud possessions of their own mother when she came to the house as a bride, and was the principal ornament of their humble living-room, as all swiftly remembered; and besides, there was that gloomy superstition which had been instilled into them since infancy, - a broken mirror meant death and disaster.

Even Sara was not proof against this. In fact, there are scarcely any of us, no matter how good and wise we may be, who do not have some such pet remnant of barbarism clinging to our souls; and Sara now stood, pale and aghast as the others, looking at that fateful, shattered glass! The baby, thus rudely awakened, set up a lively scream, which broke the spell of awed silence that seemed to have held them all until now. Molly, with a flounce of resignation, cried out, -

"Well, it's more trouble, of course, but we're getting used to it fast!"

Sara said, rather sharply, -

"Go get the baby, Molly, and be quiet, if you can; and, Morton, help me gather up the bits." While Morton, who was already down on the floor, remarked in his slow, thoughtful way, -

"I don't see what we've done, Sara, to have things keep happening so dreadful, do you?"

Sara did not know. Just then the usual sweetness of her nature seemed turning to gall. If she could have put her thoughts into words, she would have said it seemed as if some awful Thing, instead of the God of love, sat up aloft mocking at her wretchedness; and she felt for the instant, as she crossed the floor after the old broom, an impotent rage, almost scorn, of this mighty power which could stoop to deal such malignant blows against a helpless girl.

It was but a moment, - one of those fierce, instantaneous rebellions of the natural heart, which overcome us all at times of utter wretchedness, - then, just as she laid hands on the broom, there came a cry, a choked, wondering cry from Morton, - "Sara! O Sara!"

She turned; what now?

The boy, in removing the larger fragments of the glass from the boards at the back of the frame, had come across something slipped in between, and now held it up with shaking hands and shining eyes. It was a neat pile of greenbacks, laid out straight and trim, with a paper band pinned around them. Sara looked, comprehended, and felt like falling on her knees in repentant gratitude!

But, instead, she sprang towards him, and caught the package from his hands. Twice she counted it; could it be possible? Here were three hundred dollars; a sum that seemed like a fortune to the girl.

Three hundred dollars between them and suffering; and the Thing up aloft became instantly a Friend, a Father, and a God!

Molly, attempting a pirouette with the baby, now stumbled amid the *debris*, and for an instant distracted Sara's attention, as she sprang to steady her, and catch the imperilled little one from her irresponsible arms, and Morton remarked hesitantly,-

"Say, Sara, I guess I wasn't feeling just right about things, and I declare this makes me sort of ashamed!"

"Ashamed? Pshaw! Well, it doesn't me!" cried Molly, dancing about. "Now I can have a new dress, and some shoes -

"'Way hay, storm along, John,

Fannie E. Newberry

Old Stormy, he'" -

"Molly! Molly! How often must I tell you not to sing those coarse sailor songs? Now, do sit down, before you cut your feet on this glass. Morton, you see poor mother did divide that money, after all. I presume she left out just a few dollars for every-day expenses, which was what baby threw in the fire, but this must be the bulk of the money that father brought from Squire Scrantoun's."

"Yes," said Morton, still with solemn emphasis; "and perhaps, Sara, broken looking-glasses don't always mean that somebody's going to die; if they did, this would have broken last summer, wouldn't it?"

"I don't know just what to think, Morton," squeezing the baby for very joy, while this great gladness made her eyes brilliant, "only I guess we aren't forgotten, after all! I want to remember that always now, no matter how sorrowful we may be; will you help me, Morton?"

"If I don't forget myself," said her brother; "it's kinder hard to feel good when everything goes contrary, but I'll try;" and as he spoke, she saw him select a sliver of the broken glass, and, wrapping it in a bit of paper, lay it away in a drawer where he was allowed to keep his few treasures.

"Why, what's that for, Morton?" she asked curiously.

He flushed a little, then said very low, -

"It's to make us remember," and she felt that the whole circumstance must have made a deep impression on the boy.

Not so Molly. She mourned the glass because now she had no better place before which to arrange her curls than in one of the larger pieces left, which, being cracked, gave her such a resemblance to a certain old fisherman with a broken nose, who was her special aversion, that she hated to look at herself, which was, possibly, not a bad thing, for she was in danger of growing vain of her pretty, piquant face these days.

But for a long time Sara went about the humble home with a humbler heart. She felt that she had been a traitor to her Kingly Father, and took the pretty little white cross madame had sent her and pinned it up, face inwards, against the wall.

"I am not worthy to wear it," she said, "until I have done something to atone for my rebellion."

But the winter passed quietly away; and, if no opportunity offered for any great deed of atonement, there were always the little worries of every day to be patiently borne, not the least of which was a sort of nagging spirit which had gone abroad among the old neighbors and friends of the Olmstead family. Possibly they were a trifle jealous of Sara's looks and bearing; it may be those who had predicted failure for her, "because them as keeps so stiddy to books ain't apt to hev much sense at things what caounts," were disappointed that she succeeded so well, or, - let us be charitable, - perhaps they thought the children all needed a little maternal scolding on general principles; anyhow, whatever they thought, there was something unpleasant in the air.

Sara felt it keenly, and drew still farther into her shell of reticence, keeping closely to her studies and home duties, until the neighbors had some excuse for their plaints that "she didn't care for nothin' nor nobody but them pesky books!"

One day Mrs. Updyke came in, sniffing as usual, and casting a hasty glance about the room with her cold, restless eyes.

"How d'ye do, Sairay?" she remarked, loosening her shawl. "I thort as how ye mought be lonesome, so I come over an' brung my knittin' a while; you got some on hand tew, I s'pose?"

"Well, not knitting, but I've sewing," said Sara, trying to feel hospitable, and wondering what Mrs. Updyke would think if

Fannie E. Newberry

she should confess that she scarcely knew the meaning of that word "lonesome." "Let me take your hood and shawl, won't you?"

"Waal, while I set; is the babby's well as usual?" with a keen glance at the little fellow, who was happily dragging a pasteboard cart on spool wheels about the floor.

"Very well, thank you; and grows so fast! He walks nicely now, and can say 'Monnie,' and 'Mawta,' and 'Wawa,' - that's me, - besides several other words."

"H'm; got any flannils onto him?" "Oh, yes; I made some out of father's old ones," with a sigh at the beloved name.

"Ye did, hey? Hope they fit som'ers near."

She now critically examined the room once more; but as it was far neater than her own, she could not reasonably find any fault there, so started on a new tack.

"How old's Morton?"

"Twelve next summer."

"Gittin' to be a big boy, ain't he?"

"Yes, and such a good one! He is a great help to me."

"Waal, he orter be; some boys o' twelve airns their own livin', don't ye know?"

"Yes; and Morton can do something when it comes warmer, but he needs more schooling yet, though, indeed, he often does odd jobs on a Saturday that bring in a little. He's an industrious boy, and I want him to have a good education."

"Waal, as to thet, some folks thinks too much o' book-larnin', *I* say! Your fayther didn't hev much o' it to boast on, an' see what a good pervider he was. Books is well enough, but sense is better, an' forehandedness is best o' all."

As she talked, her needles clicked sharply amid the clouded blue yarn of her half-formed sock, and her eyes, almost as sharp, kept roving about, while the uneasy nose seemed determined to root out anything that might escape them. Just then Molly came in breezily, her curls flying, and her cheeks a bright pink, and, seeing the visitor, managed, all in one instant, to give Sara a lightning glimpse of a most disgusted little visage, even while she turned with a dimpling smile to say, -

"Why, Mrs. Updyke, is it you? Then that must be why Zeba Osterhaus and Betty Pulcher were crossing the street in front of your house; I guess they couldn't get in."

"Crossin' the street - where? Jest below?" beginning to wind up her yarn hurriedly. "Hed they railly been to my haouse?"

"Well, I'm not sure, but I think so; I didn't ask 'em where they'd been."

"And be they to thet little stuck-up Mis' Gurney's naow?"

"They went in there - yes."

"H'm. Jest bring my shawl, Sairay. Come to think on't, I've got an arrant there myself this arternoon - come nigh to disremembering it. Waal, good-day; why don't ye come over ever? When ye want advice, or anythin', I'm allers there," and the woman ambled swiftly away, having quite forgotten the lecture she had prepared for the "shiftless, bookish gal" she was leaving, and only intent on learning what Zeba and Betty could want with her opposite neighbor.

Molly dropped into a chair, and laughed merrily.

"Didn't I get rid of her slick, though? Say, Sara, what does she make you think of?"

"Hush, Molly, she's a good soul, and means well."

"So's a cow, but you don't want her trampling all over your garden! I'll tell you what she's like - an old rabbit in a cap. She keeps her nose going just the same, and her ears are even longer."

"Molly! Molly!"

"Well, it's so, and you can't deny it. Do you know, Sara, she stopped Morton and me this morning, when we were going to school, and told him it was a shame for him to 'set araound, a-livin' on his sister, and he ought to get a berth in one of the fishing-smacks, and would if he had any grit to him.' It made Mort as blue as anything, and he's gone down to Uncle Jabez Wanamead's now, to see about shipping."

"Molly, are you *sure?*" springing up in excitement. "I won't have it. He's too young, and hasn't had half schooling enough; and, Molly, are you certain he went there?"

Molly nodded, quite enjoying this excitement in her usually placid sister.

"Then I must go after him, and leave you to tend Neddie. Oh, *why* can't people mind their own affairs?"

Poor Sara, trembling all over, started hastily towards the wardrobe for her outer wraps, when a stamping outside the door arrested her, and in a moment the boy entered, knocking the last bit of snow from his boots as he did so.

Sara's eyes, bent upon him, discovered something in his expression which made her cry out, - "Morton, what have you been doing?"

"Doing? Why" -

"Tell me the truth!" she commanded, almost fiercely.

He turned upon Molly with sudden anger.

"Have you been tattling? I'll bet you have!"

"No, but I told Sara; you didn't tell me not to."

"Lots of good 'twould have done, if I had! You never kept a thing in your life - never!"

"Did, too, Morton Olmstead!" her pout melting swiftly into a mischievous smile.

"Well, what, I'd like to know?"

"My shell chain - so there! You've tried and tried to get it away, and you never could!" at which comforting remembrance she broke into a laugh, which was so infectious even Morton had to smile.

But he turned from her with a disdainful gesture, only to meet Sara's anxious, questioning eyes.

"Well, I've shipped," he answered doggedly, "that's what!"

"Morton!" With the word all the strength seemed to go out of her, and she dropped weakly into a chair.

"Who with?" she asked sternly, for once forgetting even grammatical rules in her intense dismay.

"With Uncle Jabez Wanamead; he's going out in a week or two, and needs a boy."

"Morton, you can't go!" a determined look settling over her white face. "It's a rough, dreadful life! Old Jabez drinks like a fish, and you'll have to mix his grog a dozen times a day; then you'll have all the dirty work to do, day and night, and be sent aloft where a cat couldn't cling, with the boat pitching like a sturgeon, and, as likely as not, be thrown to the deck with a broken arm, if you're not killed outright. And when all's said and done, you'll never be anything - *any*thing but a fisherman!"

"What else was pa?" stoutly. "Anybody'd think you was ashamed of him!"

She hesitated for a moment, and in her excitement began pacing the room, her face working with contending emotions, while the children sat still and watched her, awed into silence. At length she stopped before them, and seated herself in the chair which had always been that father's when at home, and said, in a voice so sweet and sad that it thrilled even Molly's careless little soul, -

"No, Morton, never, never ashamed of our father! Instead, I love and revere him, for he was a true, good man, - 'one of nature's noblemen,' as Miss Prue once said, - but, listen, Morton! It wasn't *because* he was a fisherman, but in spite of it; for, though it is a life that makes men brave, sturdy, fearless, and honest, it makes them also rough, profane, and careless in life and death; in fact, it develops their bodies, but not their minds or souls.

"And, O Morton, I so want you to be all that father was, and something more. I want you to be educated and refined. That Mr. Glendenning was as brave as the best of our fishermen, and dared face any storm, but how kind he was, and gentle! How respectful to poor Zeba, how thoughtful for his aunt and uncle, and what a gentleman in every way! Morton, I want *you* to be a gentleman too."

"He can't, Sara," put in Molly, her eyes big and round, "he's too poor; a man's got to have at least a hundred dollars to be a gentleman, and Morton hasn't but three cents."

Sara smiled, and the boy looked slowly from one to the other in a ruminating way.

"But everybody's twitting me with being a lazy good-for-nothing, Sara, and I can't stand it! Besides, I told Uncle Jabe I'd go, and now I've got to."

"You can't; I forbid it!" her eyes flashing. "Go at once and tell him that it is not to be thought of."

It was an unwise speech, as Sara instantly felt; for Morton, though he could be coaxed into almost anything, was worse than a mule when driven. Now the dogged look she was learning to dread settled over his face, and he squared his shoulders sturdily.

"Well, I guess you'll find I can, Sara Olmstead, and it will take somebody older and bigger'n you to stop me, too! So 'forbid' till you're tired, if you like; I've given my word, and I'm going - that's settled!"

The poor girl's heart sank like lead, and she could have bitten her unruly tongue out for those foolish words. She knew only too well that Morton would have the support of nearly all their friends in Killamet, who could see no reason why he should not follow his father's calling, and begin, like him, at the bottom of the ladder, as "the boy."

Though they knew the hardness of the life, they reasoned that it "helped toughen a youngster, and make a man of him." To them, Sara's ideas were foolish and high-flown, their notion of a "gentleman" being too often associated with city "lubbers" who came down to spy out the land - and sea - in their ridiculous knickerbockers and helmets, and who did not know a jib from a spanker, or had any idea when a sailor spoke of the "hull" of his vessel, that he referred to anything but the sum of its component parts! Gentlemen, as a class, were not held in high esteem at Killamet. Even Captain Norris laughed at fine manners, and would doubtless say, -

Fannie E. Newberry

"Oh, give the boy a chance to try his sea-legs, if he wants to - a little toughening won't hurt him."

No one but Miss Prue would thoroughly sympathize with, and stand by her, and what were she and Miss Prue against so many?

They ate their supper in a glowering silence, unusual in that cottage, even Molly for once being oppressed by the gloomy faces about her; then, still in silence, she washed the few dishes, while Sara undressed the baby; Morton, meanwhile, taking up a school-book, in which he sat apparently absorbed, until his twin, happening to pass behind him, stopped, and, with a flip of her dish-towel, cried out, -

"Why-y, Mort Olmstead, you're studying your g'oggerfy upside down!"

He gave her a scowl, but his face flushed sensitively, as he quickly reversed the book, and Sara, turning a little from the fire, where she was cuddling the baby, met his eyes with so loving and tender a look that he could scarcely bear it. Something rose in his throat, threatened to rise in his eyes too, and feeling that his only safety lay in flight, he muttered that he had an errand down town, caught up his hat and worsted tippet, and ran out of the door, nearly knocking some one over who stood upon the step. "Well, I like being welcomed with open arms," laughed a manly voice outside; "but there is such a thing as too hearty a greeting, eh, Morton?" and the boy, too dazed to speak, re-entered the room, followed by Mr. Robert Glendenning.

CHAPTER X

ROBERT GLENDENNING

Sara rose, with the now sleeping baby in her arms, and stood with the firelight playing over her noble young form, and with something - was it the firelight too? - flushing her sweet, sensitive face. She had no idea what a picture she made, nor how fair she appeared in the eyes of the young man in the doorway; for her thoughts were full of chagrin at what seemed the untidiness of the room, with baby's clothes and the children's books scattered about, and the fact that she had on an old, worn dress, instead of the Boston cashmere. For she did not realize that our most beautiful moments come from thoughts within, and are quite independent of dress and adornment, and that to-night the struggle she had been through made her expression so lovely, she had never been more attractive. She held out the hand that could best be spared from the little one's support, and said cordially, -

"I'm very glad to see you, Mr. Glendenning; are your aunt and uncle here?"

"No, Miss Olmstead; I left them in Boston, and just ran down for a day or two, before I go West once more. I - had business."

She saw him seated before she stepped to the alcove bed to lay the baby down, then, coming back, took a seat on the other side of the fireplace, and asked softly, -

Fannie E. Newberry

"Have you heard?"

"Yes," in the same tone; "Miss Zeba told me. You did not write to auntie?"

"I could not - yet."

There was a little pause, which was broken by an outburst from the other side of the room, where the children were supposed to be studying.

"I tell you 'tis too, Morton Olmstead. I'll ask Sara, now!"

"Well, Molly, what is it?" she turned to ask.

"Isn't it right to say 'seven and six *are* twelve?" Morton says it isn't."

"Why, certainly," began Sara obliviously, when the guest interposed, -

"How'll seven and *five* do, Molly? Perhaps that will suit Morton better."

Molly tossed her head at her grinning brother, pouting an instant, then broke into a giggle, as she caught the full force of the sell, and went on with her sums, while Sara remarked, -

"I am not quick at such things, Mr. Glendenning. I wish I were! You spoke of going West just now; do you go soon?"

"Yes; my home is in Chicago. I have been East nearly six months on business for my firm, and now am recalled."

She looked pensively into the fire, and he thought he heard a little sigh, which perhaps encouraged him to go on, though it was with something like embarrassment that he said, -

"I felt before going so far that I ought to make a call on some of the good people here: it may be years before I return."

"H'm," muttered Molly; "I tell you, if I ever get away I'll never want to come back."

"Well, nobody'd want to have you, either," muttered her brother in return. "A girl who can't add two simple little numbers!"

Molly contented herself with making a face at him, and the two by the fire continued their rather patchy discourse: -

"I have sometimes thought," said Sara, "that we will have to leave here now, though I haven't much of an idea where we should go, or what I could do - but I must do something soon."

He was longing to ask all sorts of questions, but dared not; instead, he leaned forward, and said earnestly, -

"Miss Olmstead, I have been thinking of that, and I want you to promise me you will not take any decisive step without consulting my aunt. If I had known - all, I would have brought her with me, but here is her latest address," producing a card. "Write her everything, and let her counsel you, will you?" She bowed her head.

"It's very kind of you all to care, and if you are sure she would not be annoyed" -

"Annoyed? What an idea! Why, aren't you both daughters of the King? Doesn't that make you sisters? I know you will not break your word, Miss Olmstead."

"No, she won't," said Molly briskly; "when she says she is going to send us to bed early, she always does it."

"Molly!" cried Sara, half-laughing, half-angry, "I think it must be your bedtime, now."

"There! That's just because you want to talk to Mr. Glendenning," whined the child. "Last night, 'cause you was lonesome, you let us sit up till nine. I don't think it's fair!"

"Well," laughed the young man, to cover Sara's embarrassment, for she had blushed like a rose at this, "I did have something in my pocket; however, as it's only for early-go-to-beders, I don't believe I'll produce it to-night."

Molly was on her feet in an instant.

"I always go to bed early, Mr. Glendenning, only when Sara wants me to sit up, like last night: you don't blame me for that, do you?"

"Indeed I don't; and seeing you're so anxious to go to-night, I think I will give it to you, after all," slowly drawing a package from the pocket of his great-coat, which was thrown over a neighboring chair. Molly grasped it, managing to get out a hurried "Thank you," under Sara's eyes; pulled at the string, whirled around a few times in search for a knife, though Morton was holding his out all the time, and finally, getting to the box, snatched at its cover - and dropped the whole thing, the bonbons inside rolling all over the floor.

"Oh, oh, oh! Sara," she screamed, dancing up and down, "they're running away! What are they?"

The young man laughed heartily.

"Only French creams and candied fruits, child; you may not like them as well as Miss Zeba's striped lemon and horehound sticks, but I thought I'd give you a taste of Vanity Fair, at least."

"Is that its name?" asked Molly, who had secured a chocolate-cream, and was now burying her little white teeth in its soft lusciousness. "Oh, how sweet! and it melts while you're tasting. Is Vanity Fair all that way?"

"Pretty much," he said gravely, with an odd look at Sara.

"Well, it's nice," she concluded, after a second taste, "but there isn't much to it; you can't *chomp* it like horehound, or wintergreen candy. *I* like to chomp!"

"I presume so, and suck lobster-claws too, don't you? The fact is, I fear your tastes are too commonplace for you to thoroughly relish these French sweeties, and I'm glad of it! Now, don't eat too much to-night, for a very little of Vanity Fair goes a great way, you'll find. And now, good-night."

"Good-night, sir. I suppose some is for Morton?"

"I left that to your magnanimity."

"My who?" bewilderedly. "Do you mean Sara? Well, then, I may as well give him half this minute, 'cause she'll certainly make me," and the two finally disappeared, Molly laboriously counting over the recovered bonbons, to be sure the division was exact.

He turned back to Sara.

"It is too much care for you," he said warmly. "Think of that boy, who will soon be beginning to assert himself, and Molly, who is enough to keep a whole family on the alert, to say nothing of the baby. How are you going to manage?"

His reference to Morton reminded her of their difference, which for a time she had forgotten, and she told him about it, adding, -

"What can I do?"

"Stand firm," he said at once. "But wait; I see how hard that will be, with the whole town against you. Let me think."

She waited, watching him, while he gazed into the fire.

Fannie E. Newberry

Finally he turned again to her.

"You spoke of leaving here, why not do so now, soon? Put it to Morton that you need his protection and help, and go to Boston. You have some means?"

"Yes." If Sara had mentioned the sum of these, the young man would have been aghast; but, accustomed as she was to the most frugal living, it seemed large to her.

"Then what is to hinder?" eagerly. "Uncle Leon will stay there this winter, anyhow; and they can find you a small flat, where you could keep house in a cosey way. Then there are things you can do at home, I am sure; things for the Woman's Exchange, say, that'll help you out."

Sara's eyes brightened. It was her dream to go out into that wider life she had read of, and this seemed her opportunity.

"What would I have to pay for such rooms?" she asked.

"Oh, that would depend on locality, the conveniences, and so on; probably from eighteen to thirty dollars, although I am more familiar with Western than Eastern rentals, but I presume that's somewhere near it."

Sara, supposing him to mean this as the yearly rental, thought it moderate enough, and went on, -

"If it were not for baby, I could teach perhaps, or go out to sew; but I'll have to wait till he's older for that."

"Would you take the baby?" he asked surprisedly.

"How could I leave him?" she returned.

"I thought perhaps - didn't your stepmother have any relatives?"

"A few; but they are not people with whom he would be happy," she said simply.

He looked at her with a puzzled face, made a move to speak, then stopped, ashamed to utter what was in his mind; ashamed to tell her that such devotion to a half-brother would hardly be expected of her, and that, freed from him, she might make a far easier start in life. Instead, he merely nodded his head understandingly, and kept silence, feeling that here was a nature not to be approached, except with care and reverence, first putting off the dust-soiled shoes of custom and worldly prudence, as unfit to enter there. After a little more talk he rose reluctantly.

"Our good Mrs. Updyke will be scandalized to see a light here after half-past nine," he remarked lightly. "Have you any word to send to Aunt Felicie?"

"Always my love and reverence," said Sara, with a touch of the old-fashioned manner that Robert thought one of her greatest charms. "And, if you think I may trouble her, I will write what there is to tell, though even Miss Prue does not know all the dreams I have had for the future."

"Why should she?" asked the young man jealously. "My aunt may not be so old a friend, but I am sure she is as good a one."

"She's more than kind! I can't understand," with a little burst of confidence, "why you are all so good to a poor fisherman's daughter like me?" They had risen, and he had shaken himself into his fur-trimmed great-coat; now he turned, hat in hand, and looked down upon her, for, though Sara was tall for a girl of eighteen, he towered well above her.

"You ask why?" he began in a quick, eager tone, then something in her calm face seemed to alter his mind, or at least speech, for he added more carelessly, "Do you think it so queer? But you forget you are a princess!" laughing lightly. "Well, good-night; it is time for me to go," and, with a more hasty farewell than he had intended, he turned, and left her standing in the doorway.

*　*　*　*　*

The next morning he was sitting before a cheerful grate fire in his aunt's private parlor at a certain hotel in Boston, his long legs stretched towards the blaze, and his chin dropped meditatively on his breast, while she, at the other end of the leopard-skin, worked busily on some fleecy white wool-work, occasionally glancing towards his darkly-thoughtful face.

"Ah, well, Robare," she said at last, "this is then your last evening here?"

He shook himself a little, sat upright, took his hands from his pockets, and, forcing a smile, turned to her.

"Yes, Aunt Felicie; and a nice way to spend it, glowering at the fire! Where's uncle?"

"He has to that meeting gone at the Natural History building; I cannot its name remember. Why? had you a private word to say?"

"Well, I haven't told you about my trip yet, to Killamet."

"Ah! It was then to Killamet that you have been? I have thought so, though you did say it was a business trip."

"And so it was, partly; old Adam has sold my yacht, and I went to get the money."

"Are there, then, no banks with drafts, or notes of post in Killamet?" rallyingly.

"Don't tease, auntie, but listen. I called on the little princess."

"Of course."

"And, Aunt Felicie, her father is lost at sea, and she is caring for all those little ones, alone."

"Ah, the poor child! Is she then born to trouble, as the sparks do fly upward? Are they very, very poor, Robert?"

"No; she said they had means, though it is probably but little, a thousand or two at most; they seemed comfortable, though you know how plainly they live; and, aunt, she is more beautiful than ever!"

"Yes, hers is of that kind of beauty that does grow, as her soul grows, for it is from the within. Did she to me send any special word?"

"Yes, her 'love and reverence;' can't you imagine just how she said it, with that little Priscilla touch which is so quaintly charming?" Then he told of Morton's revolt, and the advice he had given Sara, at her request; also the promise he had extorted.

"And now, aunt, she must have help; not only advice, but other things perhaps."

"Never from you, Robare!" sharply. "Of what are you thinking?"

"You have always let me help in your charities, auntie," he said in a wheedling tone; then, tossing back his head suddenly, "But this is different, of course; only just think, Aunt Felicie, how the poor child's hands are tied!"

"But the poor child's spirit is not, my Robare, and it is that of a free-born fisher-lass, who would not be dependent, even in its thought; leave Sara to me, my dear boy; I think it is that you may trust my discretions, is it not?"

He leaned forward, caught the pretty white hand from its flying task, crushed it against his lips, then, flushing hotly, rose

Fannie E. Newberry

from his chair, and walked down the room, ashamed of the agitation he could not suppress.

There was silence for a moment, while the perky little Bougival clock on the mantel ticked merrily, and madame's needles kept the time; then Robert broke it abruptly.

"Aunt, I'm almost twenty-four."

"Yes."

"And worth a clear ten thousand."

"Yes." "And make at least three thousand a year."

"Yes."

"And uncle and yourself are my nearest relatives."

"I am aware."

"Well, haven't I a right to please myself?"

"You haven't a right to tie yourself by your hands, and your feet, for a whimsey which may pass away. Go back to your busy Chicago, my Robare, and work hard, and live the right, pure life for one year, then tell me what is your thought."

"*Must* I, auntie?"

It was with the old boyish voice and manner he said this, and his aunt broke into a laugh, though her eyes were wet.

"You naughty child! Will you now obey your good *tante*, or not?"

"Yes, ma'am, I will; but you will keep me posted?"

"Possibly, my boy," bending carelessly over her work.

"Aunt Felicie," he strode up to her with sudden passion.

"Do not answer me so! I am a man, and I love this fisher-lass with all my heart!"

He had stopped directly before her, and she saw that his face was white with feeling. Down went the worsted-work, and, rising, she flung both arms about his neck.

"My Robare, my nephew, my son!" she cried in a choked voice, "I want the best that earth and heaven can give to you; and you - you do push over my ambitions, and expect that I will at once be glad and gay."

"But, auntie, you admire her too."

"I do, Robare; she is good and fair to see; but you must of the others take thought too, and she does need many teachings, dear."

"You'll teach her, auntie?"

"Oh, be quiet, then!" pushing him pettishly away. "Of what use to argue with a man so enamoured? Go thy Western way; obey me, and I will tell you every week all that there is to tell. Are you content?"

"I'll have to be," laughing a little at her expression; "but remember," turning in the doorway, "if I don't hear, I shall immediately find that business compels an Eastern trip." And, shaking a warning finger at her, he disappeared to his packing in an opposite apartment.

Madame Grandet, meanwhile, resumed her work, and held it till the door had closed behind the young man. Then she dropped it, her smiles vanished, and she grew grave and thoughtful; for, though far less worldly than many, she was too much of a Frenchwoman to look upon a misalliance without a shiver of dread and apprehension. Her relationship to Robert

　　　　　Fannie E. Newberry

was only by marriage, but an own child could not have been dearer, for he was bound to her by all the traditions and ties of a lifetime. His mother, pretty Nadine Grandet, had been her earliest friend, and they had lived side by side, in a little village on the Ouise, until she was wooed and won by the American artist, Robert Glendenning, who had been attracted to that neighborhood by his studies, and the fame of Sevigne, whom he worshipped afar. He finally brought his pretty French bride to America, and they lived happily in an Eastern city till the little Robert was twelve years old. Then a sudden illness took the wife and mother to heaven, leaving the husband and son to keep house in a Bohemianish way, until Nadine's studious brother, Leon, who had meanwhile married the lifelong friend of his sister, Felicie Bougane, decided to come to America.

The Grandets had no children, and as soon as the madame's eyes fell upon the little Robert, who was wonderfully like his dead mother, her heart went out to him; and from that time on he had been like a son to her, especially after his father's death, a few years later.

As the artist was unusually prudent, and no genius, by which I mean he painted pictures which the public could understand, and therefore did buy, he left a snug little sum to his son. This the young man decided to invest in Chicago, and chose architecture for a profession, two wise moves, as subsequent events proved. As for his uncle and aunt, they had no settled home, but followed wherever science beckoned, and a wild dance she sometimes led the two, as the poor little madame often thought.

But this winter certain proof-sheets anchored them in Boston; hence Robert's intense desire that Sara should make haste to settle under his aunt's protection, before some new flitting should put too great a distance between them. This devoted aunt was ready to make any sacrifice for her dear boy, but not so ready to see him make one; often a much harder thing for a loving heart.

The madame, being of Huguenot ancestry, and as sturdy a Protestant as ever lived, could have suffered martyrdom, like her grandfather of blessed memory, for the faith that was in her; but to see her boy suffer perhaps a ruined life because of one mistake in early manhood, terrified her, and she was now often sorry she had let her artistic admiration for that unusually fine head in the cottage doorway lead her to such lengths the summer before.

Sara as a pet and *protegee* was one thing; Sara as her nephew's wife quite, quite another!

But in her varied life she had learned the two wisest lessons God ever sets his children, - those of waiting and trusting. So, after a half-hour's silent meditation now, she resumed her work with a more cheerful look and manner.

"What is done is done," she said in her own tongue. "The only thing left is to make the best of it;" and when Robert returned, after completing the preparations for his journey, he would never have dreamed that she had a care upon her mind, or the least foreboding in her heart, to see her bright face, and hear her sunny laughter.

Fannie E. Newberry

CHAPTER XI

BETTY'S QUILTING-BEE

As for Sara, the interview with Robert Glendenning roused her to a new interest in her changed life, and to new hopes and plans, which are always delightful to youth; and these kept her from sinking back into that settled sadness which had been almost unnatural in one of her years. First, she wrote the promised letter to Madame Grandet, which was no light task for one so little accustomed to the use of the pen.

It began stiffly enough, but after the first few sentences the interest of her subject so occupied her, that she forgot to choose her words, and, when afterwards she read it over, she felt almost frightened at its ease and abandon.

"I'm afraid she will think it too - too - not respectful enough," she said, eying the closely written sheets dubiously; "but if I write it over I shall have to send Morton to Zeba's for more paper," and, pressed as usual by economy, she let it go without change, thereby greatly astonishing and delighting the madame. "For," thought she, "a girl who can write like that is of no common clay, and is bound to find her level. If it is to be as the wife of my Robare that she reaches it, have I any right to keep her back?"

After Sara had written the letter, her loyal heart reproached her so that she could not rest until she had also invited a talk with Miss Prue; so one fine day when there was just a hint of spring softness in the air, as delicate as the flavor in a perfect dish, she wrapped baby in his cloak, and drew him on Morton's sled to the cosey bay-windowed cottage. Miss Plunkett seemed delighted to see them, so was the parrot, who insisted on so much notice at first, that conversation progressed only by hitches; but, becoming sleepy after a time (for Miss Polly was an ancient maiden, and extremely fond of her "forty winks"), she relapsed into a grunting quiet, and, as baby was also still and happy over some blocks always kept ready for his use, the two soon became deeply engaged.

When, however, Sara had gotten as far as the removal to Boston, the elder woman threw up her hands in dismay.

"Goodness! child, of what are you thinking? Are you left so well off that you can afford even to think of this thing? Why, my dear, even I, with my means, which most Killamet people think large, would feel as if abandoned to the wolves, there! I couldn't begin to live on my income."

Sara's eyes opened wide.

"But, dear Miss Prue, I haven't so much altogether as you have in a year."

"Then, are you crazy, child? You'll feel as if cast on a desert island in that crowd of strangers, with no one to care whether you live or die; and you couldn't live six months on so little."

"But Mr. Glendenning said I could get two or three rooms for somewhere from eighteen to thirty dollars, and I hoped, with the rent of the cottage here" -

"A month, Sara, a month; surely you didn't expect to pay so little for a year!"

"Why, yes, I did; I'm afraid I'm dreadfully ignorant, Miss Prue."

Fannie E. Newberry

"As bad as a chicken just out of the shell," shaking her head with comical lugubriousness. "Go to Boston, indeed! you'd starve to death on a doorstep, all four of you, I can see you now, laid out like a row of assorted pins, for all the world. Humph! Boston, indeed!" with bridling earnestness. "Besides, what business has that Glendwing, or whatever his high-falutin name may be, to mix himself up with our affairs? I declare, Sara, I've a great mind to move the whole lot of you down here, and take care of you myself. I would, too, if it wasn't for Polly; but she'd quarrel with the children all day long, and make life a burden."

Sara laughed, but looked disappointed too.

"I see it's not to be thought of now, Miss Prue; but I hoped I could work there, and indeed I don't know what there is to do here."

"Well, there's that, of course, and I'll have to own that Cousin Nancy Prime, who lives in Hartford, always says, when I talk so, that there's no place where the poor are so well looked after as in a large city; but it seems to me just like a howling wilderness, and, besides, who wants to be looked after? I don't, nor you either; we want to have our own means, and be independent of charity."

"Yes; but it won't take so very long to finish my little capital, then what will I do if there is no work to be got? and you know there isn't any here."

"Advertise for summer boarders," said Miss Prue brilliantly. "I don't know why people shouldn't come to Killamet, as well as to fifty other places along this coast. It's only because when they get here there's no place to put them in, or, possibly, they haven't discovered our great merits yet. Our beach, and the scenery about it, are finer than those of half the places they throng, and what if they do have to come either by stage or boat the last few miles! It gives all who don't consider time, and are only off for an outing, so much the more variety. If you advertise as I've seen people do before now, you could make it seem a perfect paradise, and not be half so far out of the way, either."

"I never thought of that. *I* take boarders? How queer!"

"Well, everything's queer, that is about you; my life has been humdrum enough, we all know; but you seem marked out for exceptional fates - and fortunes perhaps."

A funny light glinted in the girl's eyes.

"I'm afraid the summer boarders would think *they* had been marked out for hard fortune, after eating my meals. What do I know about fancy cooking?"

"Nothing; and you don't want to. Most of them have got their stomachs so upset by their high-spiced Frenchy dishes that they've got to have a change of diet. You can cook fish to perfection, for I've tried you, and make good bread, and you are naturally neat and dainty, which goes for much. Take my cookbook home, and study up a few simple, nice recipes this winter, so's to be ready. Don't try for too much, but do excellently well all you undertake; and try it. You know I'll help you all I can; I believe you'll succeed!"

"But what rooms have I?"

"I knew you'd say that, and I am prepared with an answer. There is, to begin with, the spare room off your living-room."

"Oh, that?" broke in Sara, as if Miss Prue had touched on something sacred.

"Yes, just that: we all have too much veneration for our spare rooms. Now, answer me truly, of what earthly use is it to you?"

"Why, none; but mother's best things" -

"Will lie there, given over to spiders, dampness, and moths, till they fall to pieces. Use them; that's what they were made for, and, so far, they haven't fulfilled their purpose in life much better than some of the rest of us," smiling at her own conceit. "Get them out, air them, and use them; then, if needs be, and you could get boarders enough to warrant it, you could have the roof raised, and make that loft into two nice rooms; but that is far ahead yet. Take two people first, for your spare room, then get Mrs. Updyke and Mrs. Filcher to lodge a few more, and you board them. Isn't that a scheme?" with a triumphant laugh.

"If I can do it; but I'm afraid, almost."

"So am I!" with a funny look. These sudden changes of base were a characteristic of Miss Prue's; perhaps she believed, with Emerson, that "unchanging consistency is the mark of a stagnant soul." "But what else is there for you here, safe at home?"

"Nothing," discouragedly. "If there was only a canning factory, I could work in that."

"Well, there isn't, so there's no use wishing. After all, I believe my plan is practicable. Of course you are young in years, but you've had any amount of experience; then you would only take women and children, and they'd be easy with you." (O confiding Miss Prue!) "I believe I'd try it, really."

If "in a multitude of counsellors there is safety," there is often also confusion, as poor Job had occasion to experience; and Sara felt that the more she talked about her future, the less she knew what disposition to make of it. Finally she abandoned the subject with something like despair, and asked a question in regard to the neighborhood, which made Miss Prue say quickly, "Oh! that reminds me, Sara, I want you to be sure to go to Betty's quilting-bee; you will, won't you?"

"O Miss Prue! must I? You know I never liked those bees,

and now" -

"Yes, I understand all that, still I want you to go. I have reasons. You are a King's daughter; make it one of your acts of self-denial."

Sara laughed.

"That seems odd enough, mayn't I ask your reasons?"

"No; well, yes, I believe I will tell you after all. I heard two of the girls talking about you the other day, never mind who, and I didn't like what they said. The fact is, Sara, they think you feel above them."

"Oh! how can they?"

"Well, they do, and perhaps they're half right; there, you needn't color so! *I* won't say you're not above them, but you mustn't feel so. Did you ever think, Sara, that you might get up a circle of ten here?"

"Why, no."

"Well, why not? It wouldn't hurt the girls, nor you either," dryly. "Anyhow, I want you to go to this quilting, wear that pretty new dress, and be just as nice and cordial as you know how."

Sara sighed, but acquiesced. She had always obeyed Miss Prue, but this was a trial. She wondered, all the way home, just why it should seem so. Did she really feel above the other girls, that they failed to interest her? Was it pride that made her long for quiet, and her books, rather than for the society about her? Could it be she only cared for Miss Prue because she was richer and better born than the others?

"No!" she said emphatically to that last, "I should love her in rags, I'm sure; but I do like her better because she is neat and

Fannie E. Newberry

trim, and can talk intelligently about anything. I wonder if it's wrong to feel so? I must remember that being a King's daughter makes it more necessary that I should be thoughtful for all. How prettily madame explained those two words, *'Noblesse oblige'* to me. 'The nobility of my birth constrains me.' So, if I call myself one of the royal family, how courteous and kind I must be to every one, whether agreeable or not."

Thus, when the Wednesday came which was to see Betty's quilt upon the frames, Sara left baby, with many instructions, to the children; and, dressed in her best, wended her way to the low brown house in the edge of the pine grove, where Betty lived with her parents, and an overflowing household of younger children, and whence she was not sorry to go to the smaller, but less crowded cottage of young Nathan Truman, second mate of a schooner, of whom she was as proud and fond as if he had been captain of an East Indiaman, with both a town and country house. To-day the front room, which resembled Sara's, only that its furniture was far more battered and worn, was cleared of everything but a row of chairs, which followed the length of its four walls in lines as even and true as those of an infantry regiment "dressed up" to the toe-mark for inspection; and through the centre, upon the rude and clumsy frame, was stretched a quilt of wonderful construction and a blinding confusion of colors. It was a "Remembrance Quilt," Betty explained, as soon as the company had arrived and filled the funereal rows of chairs, being pieced from bits given her by all of her friends and acquaintances.

"Here," she said, indicating a point of brick-red calico which helped to form a many-rayed figure, whose round centre was in bright yellow, "is the first new dress ma had after she got merried, and here," indicating a lilac muslin with white spots, "is her weddin' gown itself. Then there's a bit of the dress 'at was found on thet gal 'twas cast ashore ten year ago; and there's a piece o' thet one 't Zeba Osterhaus hed on when she hed her pictur' took, an' these," blushing brightly, "are scraps o' my own dresses thet I ain't wearin' yet. Then there's hunderds more, but I guess you'll reco'nize most on 'em. I've pieced it 'star-pattern', ye see, - an' do ye know? - there's one thousand an' ninety pieces in thet thar very quilt!"

There was a universal cry of admiration and astonishment at this triumphant announcement.

"How long did it take you?" asked Zeba, examining the pattern and workmanship with renewed interest.

"Wall, I've been at it now this goin' on two year; kep' it fur ketch-up work, ye know."

"Wall, we'd better set to," sniffed Mrs. Updyke, fitting on a huge steel thimble open at the top; "they ain't much arter-noons to these short days, anyhow. I'll take this star, an' you, Sairay, may work on the next, so't I kin kinder watch ye. 'Twon't do to hev any botch-work on this quilt."

Sara obeyed, but not with alacrity. It only needed the added discomfort of Mrs. Updyke's supervision to make her quite wretched; but Miss Prue, at the other end, happened to look up just in time to see the disconsolate air with which the girl drew her chair forward, and called out sharply, -

"Why, what are you doing over there, Sara? I thought, of course, I could depend upon you to thread my needles for me;" and Sara, not daring to show her pleasure at this release, made a gentle word of excuse to Mrs. Updyke, and crossed the room to her friend.

"Oh, thank you!" she murmured, dropping beside the older maiden, who was chuckling slyly; "I couldn't have sewed well at all there, she frightens me so."

"Humph! Well, she needn't, for there isn't a poorer needlewoman in Killamet. There's the queer thing about that woman - she can't really do one thing well, yet her satisfaction is complete." All this in an undertone, entirely covered by the scraping of chairs, rustling of dresses, and wagging of tongues, as the company drew up to their positions around the master-piece; and still thus protected, Sara whispered on, -

"But, dear Miss Prue, tell me, isn't such a piece of work an awful waste of time? Calico is only a few cents a yard now, and it does not take such a great deal."

"But think, my child," interrupted Miss Prue with a solemn look, "these remembrances!" And, as if by chance, her finger dropped upon an ugly chocolate colored bit both remembered as having been worn by a poor crazed creature called "Silly Jane," who belonged in the county house, but spent a good deal of time wandering about the shore.

Sara burst into one of her rare laughs, and Betty called out, -

"What's the fun, Sairay? Pass it 'round, can't you? We've been a-wonderin' what you 'n' Miss Prue was a-gigglin' over!"

The idea of Miss Prue's "giggling" rather shocked Sara; but that lady answered at once, -

"And *we*'ve been wondering if anybody else would ever take the time to do such a piece of work as this."

"Oh!" cried Betty, quite complimented, "I guess there's plenty would; I enjoyed it! It's such fun, when you're j'inin' the pieces together, to call up where you seen 'em last, an' what the folks that wore 'em was doin'."

"Well, there's something in that I'll admit; but do you need a piece of my dress to recall my personality to your memory always, Betty? If I've got to cut my clothes into bits" -

"Oh, no'm," laughing; "but it's different with you. We'd all remember you, of course, but there's some, now" -

"Silly Jane, for instance? I see you've a piece of her usual gown."

Betty hardly knew how to take this, but Miss Prue looked so pleasant and kind, she laughed again.

"Wall, in course, there ain't much to remember her for; but she was about the only one in town 't I hadn't been to, so I thort I wouldn't leave her aout, ye see."

"Yes, I see," stooping to bite her thread; at which Mrs. Updyke sniffed out, -

"Wall, fer my part, I think it's a purty nice thing when a gal spends her time in sich work; she cain't be doin' anythin' wuss" (sniff), "that's sartain!"

Miss Prue laughed.

"Makes me think of Grannie Green. When her rot of a husband used to be sleeping off his sprees, she'd say, 'I'm allers so thankful when he gits real far gone, fur then I'm sure he cain't be doin' anythin' wuss.'"

"Dear me!" bridled Betty, "I hope you don't mean to compare me to thet wretched old Jed Green!"

"No, my dear; but I used to wonder, then, if he couldn't have been doing something better, - but there! It wasn't to discuss poor old Jed Green that I came here; but, first, to work on this wonderful quilt, and, second, to ask you girls why you don't get Sara to form you into a society of King's Daughters here?"

"'King's daughters?' We look like king's daughters, don't we?" tittered Dolly Lee.

"Very much," said Miss Prue, with that air of hers which made her so great a favorite, an air of *bonhomie*, almost impossible to describe. "We've been told on good authority that we are made in the King's image, so it must be true."

"Oh! - *that?*" cried Betty.

"Certainly; you didn't think we free-born Yankees - descendants of the Puritan Fathers - were going to claim relationship with any of those effete European aristocracies, did you?" with a droll look at Sara.

"N - no."

Betty, not half understanding, but fully aware of Miss Prue's drolleries, was determined not to be caught in any trap now, so kept to monosyllables; and the latter, having created sufficient interest to insure a hearing, proceeded to make her explanations in regard to such a circle.

In a small, isolated village anything which links one, even distantly, with the great throbbing world outside, is eagerly welcomed by the young. These all have their dreams, hopes, and fancies connected with this sphere on which we move, and they are usually far too wide to be contained within one square mile of territory; unless, perchance, that mile teems so thickly with humanity as to offer every possible form of comedy and tragedy. For it is not trees and hills and skies, or even the sea, which can satisfy youth; but living, breathing, suffering human nature. By and by they tire, perhaps, of the latter, and go back to nature, - in love, as they have never been with man, - but that is after disappointment has made the heart sore.

To-day the thought of allying themselves with thousands of other girls and women in the effort to do good, set every pulse to new beating, that had ever throbbed with one spark of love for the Master; and there succeeded one memorable quilting where Dame Gossip was almost entirely excluded. As they scattered for home, after Betty's nice supper, Sara found herself, as usual, at Miss Prue's side; and, looking up into her friend's face, said, with a mischievous smile, -

"So that's why you wanted me to go to the quilting, is it? If you had told me" -

"You wouldn't have gone!" interrupted her friend promptly. "I know you so well, Sara! There's a - a - well, an aloofness about you that I feel it my duty to struggle with," giving the girl a merry glance; "*some* people might call it pride, - I don't."

Sara looked troubled.

"I know you think so, Miss Prue, but I'm sure I don't feel so. What, indeed, have I to be proud of?" sadly. "Only," with more spirit, "I can't tell all I know to every one, and it bores me dreadfully to have them tell me all they know!"

Miss Plunkett laughed with enjoyment. She liked to rouse Sara occasionally; and listened with dancing eyes as the latter continued, -

"Now, yesterday, Zeba and Dolly came to call (by the way, I was reading your Ruskin's 'Stones of Venice' so think what it was to be interrupted!), and what do you suppose they talked about every minute? Why, it seems Mrs. Felcher has a brother living in Boston, who has invited her to visit him, and sent her a box of pretty things; they named over every one, even to a 'frame-bunnit covered with sating, and with a bunch of blows on top!'"

Miss Prue had grown grave.

"Yet poor Zeba could teach us both a grand lesson in cheerful patience," she said gently.

Sara crimsoned, but did not answer for a moment. They had reached Miss Prue's gate now, and the latter turned into it. "Wait!" the girl then said, almost passionately. "I am not worthy to be a King's daughter! Leave me out of your ten; tell them I can't live up to the simple requirements; I" -

"Hush! Sara," laying a hand on her young friend who was quivering with feeling, "I understand it all; you think the Lord has put you into a niche where you do not belong, for which you have no fitness. Are you sure you know more than your

Fannie E. Newberry

Maker? Perhaps He sees that, by clipping a bit here, or adding a trait there, you will be exactly the one for this niche. Why don't you try and help this beautiful plan, instead of hindering it?" Then, with a quick change of tone, "Well, good-night, daughter; remember the first meeting of our circle next Thursday: I shall depend upon you!" and she hurried in, not giving time for another word.

CHAPTER XII

NEW FORTUNES

Sara went home with slow steps, and a questioning heart.

"Am I cold and proud?" she thought. "Is it wrong to be indifferent to these petty things about me, and to love books better than people? Do I look for defects rather than virtues, I wonder? Oh, dear; how muchharder it is to *be* right than to do *right in this hard world*!"

She opened the cottage door, and saw a sight that drove away all other thoughts; for there sat Uncle Jabez Wanamead in close conversation with Morton, while Molly, open-mouthed, was holding baby, and drinking in every word. It was a great shock to Sara; for having returned to the battle with her brother, fresh-armed with authority, after Glendenning's departure, she had made such an impression upon him that she supposed he had entirely given up his dream of being a fisherman, and was now only thinking of a flitting to Boston. But, evidently, from his flushed, interested face at present all her labor was in vain. Uncle Jabez rose awkwardly as she entered, with a "Good-evenin', Sairay, thort I'd call 'round a spell."

"Good-evening," she said, constraining herself to be pleasant. "It is growing warmer out."

"Yaas, looks like a break-up, some, makes a feller think o' the

Fannie E. Newberry

Banks these days. Thort I'd see what Mort hed laid aout to do 'bout shippin' 'long o' me."

"He is not going," said Sara promptly. "I have other plans for him," with a beseeching look at the boy, who avoided her eye.

"Wall, in course, jest es ye say, but I do s'pose, ef Reub Olmstead was alive naow, his word would be go."

Sara winced. During all this struggle she had been cruelly hampered by her feeling that, possibly, she was acting entirely against what was likely to have been her dead father's wishes, and now this fear rose so strongly again as almost to paralyze her.

"If he were only here - if I could put the responsibility into his hands - if I had any one," she was saying to herself, when there came a thought that calmed her, as the mother's voice calms a frightened child. "I have a Father; why don't I put it in his hands?"

Her rigid face relaxed into a lovely smile, and, looking at her brother with the winning sweetness she could assume at times, she said, -

"I will say no more about this matter, Morton; you have only our heavenly Father to answer to now. Decide as you think is right. Uncle Jabez, will you give him till to-morrow?"

"Sartain, sartain; and, see here, my boy: I'm free to say I've urged ye to go, fur I need a clipper-built little feller like you; but I say naow, ef I hed as good a sister's you've got, I'd think twicet afore I went agin her, an' thet's the truth."

There was no mistaking his earnestness; and as he picked up his old tarpaulin, and shook hands with Sara in farewell, the respect and friendliness of his manner thrilled her with pleasure and surprise. After he had gone she talked lightly about other matters, had a frolic with Molly and the baby, helped Morton with his examples, and mended a coat of his which had come to grief, all as if there were not a care upon her mind, and indeed there was none; she had cast it on the Lord.

Morton was very quiet all the evening, but just before he mounted the steep steps to his chamber in the loft he came to her side.

"Sara," he said.

She looked up sweetly.

"I've decided." "Yes, Morton?"

"I'm going to stay at home."

"My dear, good brother!"

She drew him down and kissed him tenderly, while the tears stood in the eyes of both; and from that moment there was a new bond between them, stronger than the past had ever known.

One day some weeks later Morton came in with a large roll from the post-office, and threw it into Sara's lap.

"Ah!" she said eagerly, "it is Professor Grandet's hand; what can he have sent me?" and hurried to tear the wrapper open.

Inside were several articles in pamphlet form, two being his own composition, and the rest by another well-known scientist, all relating to the strata and minerals of this very portion of the coast. Being just then at leisure, she began one in which a certain sentence had caught her attention, and soon looked up with an air of excitement. "See here, Morton! This is certainly a mistake; and in B -'s paper, too," reading aloud a certain statement in regard to the rock formations about a mile inland. "He has, you see, made the same mistake we did at first

Fannie E. Newberry

in regard to the dip of that vein, and which we afterwards discovered to be wrong, when we came across the outcropping near the old Judd farm. Don't you remember?"

"Yes," said Morton, dropping his fish-lines to come nearer; "let's hear what he says about it."

She read him a page or two, and they talked the matter over still further; then she continued her reading, only to break out again after a little.

"Listen, Morton! Professor Grandet is with us. He isn't sure, but, from surface indications, he thinks just as we do, and the two men are having a great argument. They're going to discuss the matter next week before the Geological Society. Do you know, I'm half tempted to write Professor Grandet what we have discovered? It might make it perfectly clear to him."

"Well, I would," said Morton, going back to his lines, more interested in them than in what, had he known it, was to have a great and lasting influence on his own and sisters' lives.

So next day Sara seated herself, with an old atlas for a desk, and wrote with care and precision what she had to tell; then, directing the missive, she went to the old teapot in search of the two cents to pay its postage.

As she lifted the lid and peered in, a sigh escaped her, for the little store of silver and copper was getting low; soon it would be necessary to take another bill from the roll of greenbacks so carefully hoarded; and the thought alarmed her, for already it was greatly reduced in size; then, remembering the lesson of dependence she was trying to teach herself, she took out two of the pennies, and resolutely replaced the lid, resolving not even to think of what it was, apparently, beyond her power to remedy.

Yet she could not keep herself quite free from worry these days. Each change of season in our fickle climate means expense; and now the spring was coming on, bringing its especial needs, her feeling was often one of sick despair. It is so hard for the young to learn simply to wait; and poor Sara felt that, to make the outlay necessary for the reception of summer boarders, would actually impoverish them, and then - what if the boarders never came? The thought was appalling!

In this frame of mind she was putting on their frugal supper of dried herring, with baked potatoes and salt, a few weeks later, when Morton dashed in.

"My gracious, Sara! I believe you get more mail than even Squire Scrantoun. Just look at these!"

There was another roll, evidently pamphlets, and two letters, - one from Professor Grandet, the other in an unknown hand. She hurriedly opened the professor's, and struggled through its tangled and much abbreviated chirography, looking up finally with a pale, puzzled, yet radiant face. "I can't quite make it out. I think - it seems to say that my letter has done him much good; he says it was read before the society, and is printed somewhere."

"Perhaps it's in that paper book," suggested Molly, looking up from a shell box she was making.

"This? why, yes; I didn't think," - tearing it open. "This seems to be a Report of the Twelfth Annual Meeting" -

"Oh, do look and see if it's got your letter in!" broke in impatient Molly, springing up, and letting her shells drop in a pearly shower to the floor.

Sara turned the leaves excitedly, then stopped; and her sweet face flushed a vivid crimson.

"It is - it is here - in print - just as I wrote it; and it says, 'Letter from Miss Sara Olmstead, of Killamet, in which the vexed question is definitely settled.'"

Fannie E. Newberry

Many of us have experienced the tingling rapture of seeing our opinions in print for the first time; but it could be to few what it was to Sara, isolated, and of humble station as she was. It seemed as if that thrill of pleasure came from the very centre of her being, and tingled even to her finger-tips, while Morton and Molly, more demonstrative, if not more glad, danced about her with regular whoops of delight; after which the former mounted an uncertain chair for a rostrum, and read off the modest, concise, and clear little epistle with a flourish that ending in a crash, as the chair gave way, and landed him in the midst of Molly's shells, with crushing effect.

"Oh, oh!" laughed Sara, "do be careful;" while, with a scream of dismay, Molly fled to the rescue of her treasures.

Amid the hubub the excited girl had almost forgotten the other letter; but, as quiet was restored, she opened it, and read, with such astonishment as no words can depict, this business-like note: -

Miss Sara Olmstead:

Dear Madam, - On recommendation of Professor Grandet, after reading your letter lately published in the Twelfth Report of the M. G. and M. Society, I am empowered by the Board of Control of Dartmoor College to tender you a position in the Geological Department, as assistant to Professor Macon, in charge. The duties are not heavy, - mostly classification and correspondence, - and will only require your attendance six hours per diem. The salary is ten dollars per week. Please reply, stating your decision, as soon as possible, and address,

Yours truly,

J. G. ADAMS.

Sara looked up with something like awe.

"Morton," she said in a tone that almost frightened him, it was so solemn, "the Lord is taking care of us; we needn't have any more fear now, for we are safe with him."

I think few people sat down to a happier, though not many to a more frugal meal than theirs that night. Sara had not then a misgiving in regard to her fitness for the position; she was so filled with the impression of its being heaven-sent, that she felt, as did the apostles of old, that "words would be given her, what she should say," and wit also, what she should do. As to the salary, it seemed princely to these modest little folk; and the only wonder was, how they should ever spend it.

"But how will you manage about baby? I don't suppose they'd let him come to college," giggled Molly, with her mouth full of potato, at which she naturally choked, and had to be patted on the back by Morton, who perhaps performed the ceremony with more vigor than was necessary.

"There! there! Morton, gently dear. Now, Molly, don't speak again till you've swallowed your food. Of course I will have to find some good, trusty person to look after baby while I'm gone, for I mean you both to go to school every minute that you can."

The child made a wry face at this.

"And I just know they'll have it most a hundred weeks in a year; they always do in big cities, Hattie Felcher says so."

"No, they don't," said Morton promptly.

"Well, I guess she knows, Mort Olmstead! Her uncle lives to Boston, and" -

"Well, she don't, if she says that!" calmly boning his sixth herring.

"She does too!" red with excitement; "she was there visiting

Fannie E. Newberry

when she was a baby, and she" -

"Hush, Molly! Morton, why will you be so tantalizing? Think a minute, dear, and tell me how many weeks there are in a year; then you'll see what Morton means."

Molly, after an instant's calculation, saw the point, and shot a wrathful glance across the table.

"Well," she remarked, in a judicial summing up of the matter, "you may think you're smart, but that don't help your fare and hands from being so greasy they're just disgusting; and I don't care, so!"

"Neither do I," said Morton, calmly attacking his seventh herring, and his hot-headed little sister, as usual, was vanquished by his superior coolness and precision.

This time even Miss Prue was satisfied, and entered heartily into all the plans and arrangements for the flitting, while Morton forgot his own disappointment in the interest of this great change.

They were in the midst of the packing, Sara, Miss Prue, and Morton, with Molly guarding the baby, who had a savage desire to snatch at everything and destroy it, when the elder maiden laughed out, -

"Sara, I've a scheme; you can let the house as a summer cottage, instead of taking the boarders I once insisted upon. Now, come! Isn't that an idea?"

"If I can't sell it," said Sara.

"Of course, but then you can't. Nobody ever sells anything in Killamet except tobacco. I doubt if you could give it away!"

Sara smiled and sighed in a breath.

"I'd hate to do either, but I fear it will never be our home again, so why cling to it? But really, do you suppose any city family would be satisfied with this?" indicating the large, littered room with a sweeping gesture.

"Why not, just for the summer? They crowd into far more uncomfortable places, I'm sure. I can imagine this room with pretty rugs and cane chairs, and a hammock slung across the alcove, and a pinebough ablaze in the fireplace, being a most attractive nook some cool summer evening, after a long day of blue-fishing; and there's one nice bedroom besides the loft."

Sara shook her head dubiously.

"I wish some one would take it, but I'm afraid it will have to stay closed and useless. Molly, Molly! Do watch the baby; he's just starting for the best glass sugar-bowl with the hammer, and I think he has some tacks in his mouth."

Baby having been made to disgorge his too sharp repast, the talk ran on to other things, Miss Prue giving much valuable advice on "How to live on ten dollars a week;" but the sage maxims were so interspersed with hammerings, hunts, and hurry, that I fear much of their value was lost on Sara.

It happened to be a fair day when they left for the new home, and it seemed as if all Killamet turned out to bid them God-speed. They ate their last dinner with faithful Miss Prue, then, accompanied by a goodly little procession, walked down to the beach, where Jasper Norris, who had somehow happened home a few days before, was waiting with his tidy little wherry to row them across the bay to Norcross, where they would reach the railroad, their goods having been sent by wagon a day or two before. It was curious to see how differently each of the Olmstead group was affected by this leave-taking.

Sara was pale and still, and her beautiful, sad eyes heavy with unshed tears; Morton had an air of manliness new and good to see, and seemed determined to look after every one and everything; Molly's cheeks were red, and her eyes aglow with excitement, as her feet danced over the white sand, while baby laughed at the surrounding friends with charming impartiality, and talked every minute in his own particular dialect, which eye and motion made almost as intelligible as the queen's English.

At length they stood on the crescent beach, the sea rolling in at their feet, as Sara had watched it so many times. A fresh April wind curled the waves into fluffy white turbans (as Molly observed), and an April sun gave them an almost blinding sparkle. Each lighthouse gleamed whitely across the bay, and the tall cliff rocks stood out in bold relief against the dazzling blue of the sky; but Jasper saw it all as through a mist, for his heart was heavy.

What did this departure portend? Would it break up their life-long friendship? He was glad to see his mother take Sara's hand, and, as she kissed her tenderly, exact a promise that she would write occasionally.

But when the others crowded around, each eager for the last word, he turned away and busied himself with his tiller-rope, sick at heart. At last the good-bys were all said; Morton had taken his seat at the rudder, and Molly was nestled with baby on a cushion in the bottom of the taut little boat, when, just as Jasper was holding out a hand to help Sara aboard, she turned and gave a last, long, lingering look over the quaint little town in its radiant setting of sea and sky.

"Good-by, all - all I love!" she said brokenly, then turned to Jasper, and was soon silently seated in her designated place.

The young man, also silent, took up the oars to fit them into the rowlocks, when suddenly Molly was seen scrambling to her feet.

"Wait, Jap, wait!" she cried eagerly, and leaping over the seats, sprang lightly ashore.

"Why, what is it?" "Have you lost something?" "What can the child want?" were some of the questions showered after her from boat and beach, as she was seen to stoop and plunge a quickly bared arm into the water.

She drew it forth again, and held up something green and many-clawed.

"It's just a lobster I saw," she said calmly, as she climbed back to her place with the surprised crustacean gingerly suspended from her dripping hand. "We can boil it to-morrow, Sara, then I'll have the claws to suck; where shall we put it so't it won't grip the baby?"

The laughter called forth by this characteristic escapade effectually dispelled all tears and sadness.

Even Jasper grinned, as he handed the creature on to Morton, to be thrown into the bait-box under the stern-seat, and, amid lighter sallies and laughter, instead of tears, they rowed away. But Sara's eyes rested upon her well-loved birthplace until they had rounded the lighthouse, and the familiar scene was quite shut out by the intervening tongue of land.

It was about mid-afternoon when the little party entered the railway coach at Norcross; and this being Molly's first glimpse of a train of cars, her eyes would have put an owl's to shame for size and roundness, as she sat on the very edge of the seat, and stared uneasily about her.

Jasper, having fixed them comfortably, gave a hurried hand to each, leaving the last for Sara. He had thought a dozen times just what he would say to her at parting, but everything went out of his head in the nervousness of that last anxious moment, with the engine apparently determined to run away with all who would linger over their farewells, and he simply uttered a choked "Well, good-by, Sairay!" as he held her hand an instant in a trembling clasp.

Fannie E. Newberry

"Good-by, Jasper, I shall not soon forget your kindness; but do hurry off before the train starts." So does the rush and rattle of modern times overpower romance and sentiment.

But, safe on the station platform, he watched the one window he cared for with misty eyes, while Sara on its other side felt that the last of home was leaving her, while before her stretched only a strange, untried, uncertain future.

CHAPTER XIII

FROM KILLAMET TO DARTMOOR

The train started with a shriek, faintly echoed by excited Molly, the bells clanged, belated men swung themselves up to the rear platform, there was the quick panting of impatient haste through the monster's whole length, till the jerks settled into a contented glide, and Molly's distressed puckers broadened into a smile of delight.

"It's like flying!" she gasped, turning from her intent gaze out of the window. "Everything's flying, only the trees and fences all go the other way. I tell you I like it!"

Dartmoor was about a three hours' ride distant, so it was not yet dark when they reached there, and were met by Madame Grandet, who had been in the college town with her husband for a fortnight. How good it was to see her charming face again! Sara felt the stricture of forlornness and fear about her heart loosen suddenly at sight of her.

"Here are you all then, quite safe and well!" she said merrily, as she took the baby from his sister's tired arms, "and I have a carriage for you; pray follow." They obeyed; and soon the party were driving through the broad, quiet streets, bordered by old elms and maples whose summer foliage must stretch a green canopy quite across them, thought Sara. She gazed about her, and was delighted with the comfortable, old-time look of the deep-verandaed houses, set solidly in the midst of green

Fannie E. Newberry

lawns, outlined by winding shell walks of dazzling whiteness.

Once she uttered a cry of pleasure, as they crossed a large green park interspersed by broad avenues, with a pile of gray stone buildings surrounding three of its sides, while elms of rare height and grace were scattered irregularly over its velvety surface.

"It is the campus that you now see," said the madame, answering the question in her eyes, "and those large buildings are of the college a part. Do you observe over this way, to our right, a wide, wide arch with a statue above? It is the entrance to the museum, in which you do work, and this beautiful street we drive upon, it is the College Avenue, and here are the homes of the faculty that we now pass."

"Do we live with the faculty?" inquired Molly, whose neck seemed in danger of dislocation, so constantly did she keep it twisting and turning.

"Ah! no, hardly so," laughed the madame; "it is on a little street that I do find apartments for you, but it is nice there; I do hope you will be pleasured."

"Oh, I'm sure we will! Baby dear, don't chew your pretty cloak-strings, you will spoil them. Ah! is this the place?" as they whirled around a corner and stopped shortly in a narrow but clean court, surrounded by small, trim cottages with tiny squares of green in front.

The madame led them up a gravelled foot-path - there were no fences - to a door in one of these, which she opened and entered.

"Follow, follow!" she called out merrily, and flitted up the narrow, uncarpeted stairway. She stopped at the head of this, and stood till all had gathered about her in the dim little hall-way, then, with a graceful flourish, cried, "Behold then!" and threw wide a door.

There was a universal shout of satisfaction, which made the madame's eyes dance, while Sara's grew misty with feeling; for that kind little Frenchwoman had almost settled their rooms for them, doing all an outsider could do, so that the bare, homeless look many of us can remember when newly entering a tenantless house, was quite removed.

After the first pause of surprise, the children began running wildly about, while the madame and Sara took it more leisurely. "See," said the former, "it is here your sitting room, with three pleasant windows, and a bit of a fireplace under this wooden mantel. When it is dressed with something bright it will not so bare seem. Here are two cosey bedrooms with the air and light, and a so large closet between, besides this cunning little bath-apartment, which I know you will much prize. Then here," throwing open a door, "is your kitchen, with two fine windows, and this tiny range. Is it not pretty?"

She ran about, showing its conveniences, and explaining how these apartment-cottages were built by a humane society, to furnish comfortable homes for those who had little means, ending: -

"And the rent, my dear, it is so small - so very small - only a little ten dollars a month!"

It did not seem small to Sara, but she would not damp the madame's enthusiasm by saying so; and in time she learned to appreciate, and be grateful for, this really cosey flat at so low a rental.

"The family below is very nice," said madame; "their name it is Hoffstott, and he is a little German baker of much baldness on his head, but greatly smiling and pleasant; the wife is about the same in her width as she is in her height, and laughs with a big mouth, and white teeth fine to see; and they have two little girls with yellow braids, like that candy of molasses Miss Zeba did have in her windows - and all so clean! Ah!" with a charming gesture, "it do shine through every room with soap

Fannie E. Newberry

and sand, and the brush that scrubs!"

"Dear me!" sighed Sara, "I'm afraid I can never suit them then; baby will get things around so!"

"Never do you fear of yourself, little princess!" tapping her gently on the shoulder. "I can still in my mind see your beautiful white floor and shining window-panes, down there by the sea. You, too, are clean, my sweet child, I know! Now, have you any supper had?"

"Why, no, not a bit!" laughing. "I had almost forgotten."

"Well, I hadn't," said Morton, "I'm about starved!"

"I, too!" cried Molly, and the baby put in a pathetic plea for "bed-e-mik" that was irresistible.

"Ah, such fun!" cried the madame merrily, as she whisked off her wraps. "I did think it would be so, and I had that good Hoffstott to send us a nice little tin kitchen that I now have hidden away in the warm oven; and see! I did take some dishes out of the barrel. We will have a supper to make a *chef* rave with envy soon!"

If it would hardly produce so dire an effect on a head-cook, it certainly gave supreme satisfaction to the partakers; for in the tin kitchen, which seemed to prying Molly like some Fortunatus box, was a dear little pot of baked beans, some steaming rolls, and potatoes baked in their jackets, while from a cooler place came a dainty glass of jam, and some cake.

It was now dark, and the children felt surrounded by wonders. As Molly expressed it, "Madame just turned a handle, and the light shot out; and turned another, and the water fell out;" and she asked, innocently enough, if, when they wanted milk or tea, all that people had to do here was just to move a handle, and let it run out of the wall! But madame, after her laughter, answered this by proceeding to steep some tea in an odd little contrivance over the gas-jet, much as Sara did over the log-fire at home; but neither Morton nor Molly would have been surprised to see food come sliding in, all cooked, or clothes all made, by the simple turn of a crank, so like fairyland was it all.

When, at length, the kind madame left them, Sara looked about her with an odd feeling, half forlorn, half thankful.

It was certainly a snug little haven, yet everything was so new and strange she felt as if she could never get used to it. But, during the next day or two, which was passed busily, getting the rooms into better shape, she gradually grew accustomed to the odd contrivances, and acknowledged their convenience. Mrs. Hoffstott came up, and kindly offered her services, and the baby took such a fancy to the good-natured German woman that he would hardly leave her for any one but Sara.

As to the little girls, they fraternized with Morton and Molly at once, and introduced them to their home below, and their father's shop on a neighboring street, before the day was over.

By Sunday morning - their flitting had been on a certain Thursday - everything was in excellent order, and Sara had begun to feel that the little flat was indeed home; so the blessed day was spent in the quiet and rest they all needed. As they sat around the tiny grate in the twilight, Morton looked slowly all about him. The room was square, with a large double window in front, and a single one at the side. By the madame's suggestion, and with her help, these windows and the mantel-shelf had been prettily draped with inexpensive material, which was, however, delicate in tint and pattern. Upon the floor was the only carpet Sara owned - old-fashioned, and perhaps too bright for artistic tastes, but looking warm and comfortable that chilly spring evening. Then there was a table, also draped, while the collection of minerals was conspicuous upon a set of shelves in one corner; and about the fire were a few home-cushioned chairs. Plain, to homeliness, as it was, yet the effect was so entirely one of brightness and comfort that Morton broke out with, -

Fannie E. Newberry

"Well, Sara, this is pretty nice! Rather better than Uncle Jabez's old cabin on the Mary Jane, isn't it?"

"I'm so glad you think so, Morton! And I'm sure you will like school here. Mrs. Hoffstott has taken such a fancy to baby that she will take care of him for me until I can find some one else; so tomorrow we begin our education, - you and Molly and I."

"You, Sara? How funny! Why, you are through with yours, aren't you?"

"No, Molly, I sometimes think I am just beginning; and if you dread the starting in to-morrow, so do I! Bring the Bible, Morton, and let's read a chapter, to give us courage for the ordeal."

It was indeed an ordeal! After starting off the children, with the little Hoffstotts to pilot them, and seeing baby happy with some toys in their mother's trim kitchen, Sara put on her modest wraps, and walked briskly, not giving her courage time to weaken, from the little court toward College Avenue. At its farther end she was to meet Professor Grandet, who lived there in a professional boarding-house of intense respectability and learning, from whence he was to accompany her to the museum, a programme which had been arranged with Sara by himself and madame, when they had called Saturday evening.

She found him awaiting her in the doorway, beside his wife, who greeted her with a cheery word, and bade her, laughingly, have no fear, for she knew all about professors, and really, in most things, they were no wiser than common people! Then, laughing mischievously in her husband's face, she gave him a little push down the steps, which came near upsetting both his balance and his dignity. But before he could turn to remonstrate she was volubly bidding him not to go off into a brown study over some plesiosaurus, and forget all about his charge, or make a mistake and introduce her to the dino-therium, instead of Professor Macon; then, gayly waving her hand, she vanished behind the closing door.

"She has ze spirits zat are high - she!" he said with a smile, for everything this bonny wife did seemed good to him. "It is ze best sing zat it ees thus, for she ees much alone - *la pauvre petite!* Now, I must zis sing say to you, Mees Sara; it will not be allowed zat you keep zat mos' fine colleczione while ze college have you in employ - zat ees contraire to ze rule. What would you with it then? If you it will zell, I s'all be mos' happy to buy, eh?"

"Certainly, if it is against the rule to keep it; but that seems queer!"

"But no, it ees quite right, you zee? Ze collecziones mus' be for ze college - all - no private ones; it will not do."

"Yes, I see; all must work for the general good when making a collection."

"Yes, yes, it ees so."

They were now passing into the museum building, whose wide and lofty corridors sent a thrill of awe through the impressionable girl. Feeling very small and young, she followed the professor over the tiled floors, then through two or three large apartments filled with strange looking beasts and birds of a startling naturalness, past long glass cases, where she caught hasty glimpses of everything possible in shell, bone, stone, or mineral, then across a narrow corridor, where the professor stopped and tapped at a door.

"Enter!" was called loudly from within, and they obeyed.

It was a bright, sunny room they stepped into, not large, in comparison with those they had passed through, though here, too, were smaller glass cases, as well as tables heaped with jars and specimens, and two knee-hole desks of fair size.

From one of these a gentleman advanced; not a large man, but having a fine head and face. His black hair was thrown carelessly back from a broad white forehead, while his mouth and chin were concealed under a full dark beard. His eyes, of the same dusky hue, peered keenly through glasses.

"Professor, here I have mine leetle vriend, Mees Sara Olmstead; and zis, Mees Sara, ees ze good man with whom you do vork, Professor Macon."

The professor and his new assistant shook hands, while the latter felt she herself was being classified and labelled by those penetrating orbs.

"I'm happy to meet Miss Olmstead; pray be seated. Don't hurry away, Professor Grandet; can't you sit down a while, also?"

"Not zis morning, t'anks; I haf mooch to do. Well, Mees, I leaves you in good hands; *au revoir.*"

"Good-morning; and thank you," said Sara timidly.

"Thou art mos' velcome; adieu!" and with a flourish of his hat he was gone.

"You may take off your wraps in here, if you please, Miss Olmstead," said Professor Macon, leading the way to a small cloak-room; then, as she returned unbonneted, he pointed to the desk near his own.

"This is your place, and for this morning your work will be labelling these specimens. When you are the least uncertain about one, speak to me, please. You will find everything needed before you." He returned to his own work, and Sara soon grew absorbed in hers; for it was the kind of task she liked, and had often spent hours over, for pure amusement. How it brought back the shore and the cliffs! The long rambles inland, also, and the evenings on the floor amid her specimens, down before the drift-wood fire. She forgot her surroundings finally, so interested was she; and once the professor, glancing up, smiled a little at sight of the bent head and eager, intent face. He watched her, unperceived, for some seconds, then, with a nod of satisfaction, returned to his own labors.

The three morning hours passed as one in this congenial labor, then there was the brisk walk home to meet the children at a light lunch, and look after baby. She found the little fellow supremely contented with his new quarters, having made loving advances to a gray kitten who, though suspicious of his favors, was too meek to escape them; and Mrs. Hoffstott declared he had been "so goot as nefar vas!" The older children were voluble over their school, Morton talking most of the great, cheerful rooms, with their wonderful conveniences for study; while Molly expatiated at large over a little girl with the euphonious name of Henrietta May Hendrington, with whom she seemed to have fallen rapturously in love!

Half-past one found them all at work again, and the afternoon hours were even shorter than those of the morning to all but baby, who began to grow homesick towards four o'clock, and who could not be comforted, even by the children, who were out of school at three. He wanted his "Wawa," and no one else. It was really pathetic to see how the little fellow clung to her, hiding his pretty wet eyes in her neck, and lovingly patting her shoulder, as he crooned his wordless reproaches in her ear, and Mrs. Hoffstott, looking on, thought this must indeed be a good sister to win such hearty affection, and felt her own motherly heart warm to the forlorn little orphaned brood. But, as Sara climbed the steep staircase, with the child clasped close, and opened the door of their little snuggery above, her heart was full. How had the loving Father cared for his children! Here she was, a princess indeed, in her own domain, surrounded by her loving subjects; and when she shut the door she seemed to shut out sorrow and care, for here all was peace.

How they enjoyed the nice hot supper, and the visit afterward, baby in Sara's lap, warming his pink toes before the bit of a blaze, which these chill nights of early spring demanded! Then, when the little fellow was in bed, out came the books, and all

Fannie E. Newberry

was still, as Molly hunted out lakes and rivers, Morton puzzled over fractions, and Sara revelled in Owen, ready at any moment to give her help to the younger ones.

Perhaps some dainty miss of eighteen, enjoying her first winter in "society," and counting up her bouquets and admirers after last night's party, might think it too tame an existence; but to Sara, reared amid toil, privation, and loneliness, it was a veritable bit of Eden.

It could not be expected that such a beautiful girl as Sara could cross the campus several times a day, and pass unobserved by the hundreds of students who felt this to be their special stalking-ground; and finally, one morning when an unusual number of graceless young "Sophs" and "Freshes" were on guard there, she was subjected to so many stares, smiles, touchings of the hat, and half-heard remarks, that she entered the workroom with flushed cheeks and a perturbed manner which could not well escape the professor's keen eyes.

"You have walked too fast, Miss Olmstead; there is no such hurry these sunny mornings."

"It isn't that, sir; I - it is not agreeable crossing the campus."

"Ah!" with a lift of the eyebrows and a quizzical look at the lovely disturbed face before him. "I can well believe it! Well, there's a better way, if you would like to try it; at least a more secluded one," giving her a keen glance. "When you come down College Avenue, watch till you see a large brown house with a tower, and a porch with heavy pillars" -

"Oh, yes, sir; and a deep green lawn in front; I've often noticed it."

"Very well," smiling agreeably, "that's my home. Turn in at the carriage-drive, and follow it until you see an opening in the hedge; go through, and keep to the little foot-path; it will bring you here, for it's my own private way."

"Thank you," said Sara, "I will be very glad to use it," and seated herself at her desk in the business-like way she was acquiring, much to the professor's secret amusement.

That noon, as he sat opposite his wife at table, he said, -

"Marian, I want you to look out of the window about a quarter past one, and you will see a *rara avis*."

"Goodness! Henry, you're not having any of those horrid dinornis things brought to the house, are you?"

He laughed.

"No, my dear; this rare bird I have in mind is simply a handsome girl, who doesn't enjoy being stared at by the students, - in a word, my little helper, Miss Olmstead, - and I've told her to travel by my own cross-roads, because she comes in all of a flutter, mornings, after running the gantlet of those college scamps on the campus."

His wife gave a quick, appreciative nod. She was a pale, dark-eyed woman, with a face of rare intelligence and sweetness.

"Indeed I do want a peep at her, Henry; she's the fisher-girl with the family on her hands, that Madame Grandet told us about, isn't she?"

"Yes, the same; let me give you another croquette, wife." "No, thanks; I've sufficient. And how does she appear, very provincial?"

"Not at all, that I can see, unless to be modest as a violet, and business-like as a night-editor, be provincial. She speaks good English, and sensible, too, in a peculiarly pleasing voice, and has the most finished manners, to my notion; for she goes quietly about her affairs without fuss or remark, and says what there is to say in brief, clean words. No, she is anything but *outre*."

"Really, my dear, I never heard you praise a woman so highly before."

He smiled quietly.

"I neither praise nor dispraise, Marian; they are, with one notable exception simply out of my ken, ordinarily; but I like this little girl, where she is, unusually well."

"Be sure, then, I shall watch for her with all my eyes! Don't forget your papers, dear; oh, and turn your pockets inside out at once, please, till I see if you have any of my letters yet undelivered!"

He obeyed with a matter-of-course air, which showed this to be a common occurrence with the absent-minded scientist, and having yielded up two dainty, square missives, which he had not carried more than two days, took his departure.

An hour later Sara turned in at the designated carriage-drive, and followed its windings up near the house, then off towards the dividing hedge, never seeing two bright, interested eyes which were peering through the filmy lace curtains, and taking pleased note of her trim, erect figure in its black dress, and lovely, thoughtful face, below its plain straw hat; then passed through the hedge, and, with all the delight of a child exploring some bit of woodland, followed the well-worn little path, which crossed a corner of the next yard, then skirted a tennis-court, wound by a rather suspicious-looking dog-kennel, then led into an unused grassy lane, reminding her so gently of home that she longed to linger; but, pressing on in her narrow way, she finally brought up before a gray stone pile, in which was a small door, and, opening it with some caution, found herself in the tiny square entry just back of the familiar cloak-room.

Professor Macon took in her pleased face at a glance.

"You liked my little by-way?" he asked.

"Immensely!" with a hearty accent. "May I always use it?"

"Most assuredly!" and without more words both bent to their absorbing tasks.

CHAPTER XIV

NEW FRIENDS, NEW DUTIES, AND A NEW LOSS

The sale of Sara's collection to Professor Grandet brought her a neat little sum, with which she added a few much-needed articles of furniture to her rooms, making them more modern and comfortable; and through Mrs. Hoffstott she finally succeeded in finding a trusty little girl, who was glad to come during the hours of Sara's absence to tend baby and do the left-over bits of work for the pittance she could afford to pay. Even this left a perilously small amount for the house expenses, and the clothing of the four; but the latter necessity was made easier by Madame Grandet and Miss Prue, both of whom found they had many articles too good to throw away. The latter had pressed enough of these upon Sara, during the packing, to make Molly and herself quite comfortable, for, as Miss Prue always wore black, her dresses were suitable now; and, the madame had come to the rescue with some of the professor's cast-off trousers for Morton's use.

It was one Saturday afternoon, and Sara, consequently, at home by three o'clock, when she stood, armed with a pattern and some formidable-looking shears, about to attack a light gray pair of these, when there came a quick little "rat-tat-tat" at the door.

"Open it, Molly," she said abstractedly, thinking it might be either Kathie or Grisel; but instead of the round pink and white face and yellow braids she looked for, there appeared a tall lady, richly dressed, whose pale, fine countenance was quite unfamiliar.

The lady advanced.

"This is Miss Olmstead, I know; and I am Mrs. Macon. I have often seen you through the window at home."

Sara greeted her with a blush, and drew forward the best chair, inwardly experiencing a deep regret that she had not changed the baby's pinafore, and had kept her cutting operations in the parlor.

Mrs. Macon, however, seemed to notice neither, but praised the baby's pretty rings of hair, saying he reminded her of one of Raphael's cherubs, and asked Molly about her school, taking in, with evident amusement, the child's original answers, and little twists and tosses, till Sara could recover her equanimity, and be her own quiet self once more. Then she turned to her with some word of commendation for her laborious life, and added, with a light laugh, -

"You looked quite fierce with your great scissors as I came in. It wasn't the baby's hair you thought of cutting, I hope?" "Oh, no, indeed! I wouldn't cut his dear little curls for anything! I was trying to - to cut out some pants for Morton."

"You poor child! What a genius you must be to attempt it! Do you think you can?"

The tone of perfect *camaraderie* seemed to drive away the last vestige of Sara's shyness.

"I have once or twice at home, but it's different here: the boys dress better, you see, and Morton's getting very particular. I've a good pattern, but I do feel a bit frightened to put my scissors into the goods."

"Of course you do," rising, and going over to the table to look

Fannie E. Newberry

at the pattern pinned carefully over the old garment. "But, my dear, couldn't you cut to better advantage by turning this a little? Here, let me show you."

With a rapid movement she unfastened and cast aside the jetted lace wrap she wore, and filling her mouth with pins, after the manner of womankind, began mumbling her explanations, as she turned and twisted the paper about, Sara, meanwhile, looking on with the earnestness of a priestess of Athene, listening to her oracle.

Months of meeting in fashionable parlors could not have made them so intimate as those ten minutes over that pattern, while their heads bobbed together, and their tongues ran on in unison. For when it was adjusted, Mrs. Macon insisted on superintending the cutting, and when this was satisfactorily accomplished, to the exclusion of the one worn place, and the ink-spatters, she was as elated as Sara herself.

"There! We've done it, we've done it! Now, if you only get them together right; you're sure you'll remember which is the front, and which the back, and when you stitch them - where's your machine?"

"I haven't any," said Sara.

"Dear heart! And were you going to sew those long seams by hand?"

Sara nodded deprecatingly, as much as to say she knew it was wrong not to have a machine, but she couldn't help it; and her visitor was so charmed with the look in her sweet eyes, that she gave her cheek a playful little tap as she said, -

"It's not to be thought of! I've an excellent machine which stands useless half the time; you shall come and learn to use it: this will be just the thing to begin on. Why can't you come now? I'm anxious to see them underway, and, besides, I haven't a doubt Morton needs them; boys always are needing new trousers!"

Sara had to acknowledge that he did; and the upshot was, that in less time than it takes to tell it, baby was turned over to Molly, and Sara, with her bundle, found herself in Mrs. Macon's carriage, riding home with her, to the astonishment of the coachman, who had been preparing his mind for a long, sleepy afternoon on the box, while his mistress consulted her list, and made her formal visits. The fact is, she had forgotten all about them; just now the most interesting thing in her rather monotonous life was Sara and those trousers. An acquaintance begun in this manner could never be quite formal again. Mrs. Macon was warm-hearted, and often-times weary of doing nothing in her great silent, childless house. She adopted Sara and her little brood from that moment, and to be adopted by Marion Macon was to fall into good and gracious hands.

She led Sara, now, straight to the sewing-room, in which was the machine, throwing wide the blinds of the broad window before which it was placed.

"Did you ever use one?" she asked anxiously, as she removed the cover.

"Yes, once or twice. Miss Plunkett had one."

"Miss Plunkett; that's a name I know. I have heard my mother mention a Captain Plunkett she knew as a girl; they were a good family, the Plunketts. Then you know them?"

Sara spoke of the life-long friendship between that family and her own, but in so modest a way that the lady's respect for her increased with every word; but both were too intent on business to give much time to genealogy.

Sara proved an apt learner, and soon was making the treadle fly, while her hostess, seeing her well underway, ran down-stairs for a time. When she came back Sara had performed the cunning task of getting the pockets in place, and was finishing off the long seams.

"How rapidly you work!" cried her new friend. "My husband told me how business-like you were."

"Did he say so? I'm glad he thinks I am!" cried Sara, much pleased. "It would be so annoying to a man like him if I were not."

"And why to him especially, Miss Olmstead?" asked the wife curiously.

"Because he is absorbed in his work, and cares for nothing outside. In fact, one always is with that work," enthusiastically; "it takes your whole being for the time."

"Yet the last girl he had was a dreadful little idler, and would interrupt him in the midst of his most interesting researches to ask the silliest questions."

Sara shook her head mournfully. "I don't see how she could!"

"Well, to tell the truth," bending forward confidentially, "isn't it awfully dry and uninteresting? There! I wouldn't dare lisp it before my husband, but isn't there a good deal of - of - well, humbug, about it?"

"Humbug!" Sara's eyes glowed. "That's because you haven't studied these things, Mrs. Macon. Think, think what it must be to have your husband's power to peer into the past!

"Think of taking two or three bones, and from them constructing an animal now extinct; or, think of knowing from an impress on a stone, made years ago, what animal had walked over its then soft surface. Humbug! oh, Mrs. Macon!"

The lady laughed.

"Well, don't for mercy's sake, ever hint that I suggested such a thing; I see you're nearly as far gone as Henry himself. But, as for me, I must say I can't get specially interested in post-pliocene things, when there's so much going on around us; and how you, with all those children to look after, and their clothes to make, can care for fossils and bones, and bits of rock and mineral, is a conundrum to me."

"I hope I don't neglect the children for the bones," said Sara, so deprecatingly that Mrs. Macon laughed again.

"Don't worry about that! They look all right, anyhow, what I've seen of them. Now come, it's getting too dark to sew, and you have these nicely together; fold them up, child, and come down-stairs with me."

This was the first really elegant house Sara had ever entered; and as she followed the lady over the soft carpets, past bronze and marble, into a beautiful room, through whose western end, wholly of glass, came a rosy glow from the setting sun, she could hardly keep back her cry of delight. It was the dining-room, and seemed dazzling to Sara, with its rich tones in wall and rug, its buffet a-glitter with glass and silver, and its green garlanded windows; but her native instincts were nice, so it was only in her eyes that this astonished admiration found expression.

Mrs. Macon made a careless gesture towards the table, which was partly laid.

"Sit down, my dear," she said, "and we will have a bit of a supper together; Mr. Macon has gone into the city, and won't be back until a very late dinner. How do you take your tea, please?"

It was a delectable little spread, nearly all the dishes being novelties to Sara, even the familiar lobster being scarcely recognizable in its Frenchy dress; but she felt the refinement and delicacy of it all, as an infant feels the softness of velvet, not comprehending, only enjoying.

In speaking of it afterwards to the children she remarked, -

"I can't tell you what it was, for I have eaten meals I really relished better; but it was there, and I have never experienced it anywhere else, not even at Miss Prue's. It seemed as if I were in a palace, with soft music and sweet odors about me; yet there was no music, and the only fragrance was from the tea. No, I can't tell what it was; but sometime - *some*time, Molly, I hope you will feel it too!"

"Well, if it's going to make me feel solemn and creepy I don't want to," said that young damsel with decision. "That's the way I felt the first few Sundays in the church we go to here; it was so big and high, and had so many colors on the walls, and such dark, purple corners. I kept expecting something to happen; but I'm getting over it a little, for nothing ever does, you know, except the preaching and singing. Only, Sara, that reminds me: there's one thing I've been going to ask you about this ever so long; are the singers all hunchbacks, like Zeba Osterhaus?"

"Dear me! no, Molly, I hope not. What a question!"

"Well, then, what makes them hide so behind those red curtains? I've tried and tried to see if they were like other folks, but I couldn't; and if they are, I don't see why they act so queer!"

Sara tried to explain, but Molly evidently still held to her original opinion; there was some mysterious reason for their modesty, else why did they not stand out plain and high, as did the village choir at home? And it was many weeks before she could be moved from her stand in the matter.

Sara's work went on much the same after the close of the collegiate year, though now Professor Macon was away a large part of the time; yet, as he was constantly sending home cases of specimens, she was usually kept nearly as busy as before. But one day, sitting at her desk with only a few unimportant odds and ends of work before her, her thoughts drifted away, and soon formed themselves into words and sentences which seemed clamoring for definite expression. She seized her pen and some blank paper, setting them down as rapidly as possible, and before she quite realized what she was about had written several pages. Finally, stopping to glance over her work, she felt encouraged to continue it, which she did till her working-hours were over. That night more thoughts came to her, and the next day she completed the article. Reading it over, and correcting it carefully, she decided to copy it; and, while the impulse was upon her, even had the audacity to enclose it in an envelope and send it to a certain magazine having scientific tendencies, which came to the museum regularly.

It was an article describing some oolitic formations she had been much interested in when at the old home; and she told of her ramblings, speculations, and discoveries, in a modest, face-to-face way which gave them a certain interest in addition to their scientific value.

Several days passed, and she had given up her fledgeling for lost, when one morning she saw amid the mail upon the professor's desk an envelope addressed to herself, and opening it found with astonishment that it was an acceptance of her sketch, enclosing a check for what seemed to her a large amount. That, she often said afterwards, was the proudest moment of her life. Her whole frame thrilled with keenest satisfaction, her whole soul was uplifted in thanks for this gift that seemed directly from above.

The professor, back from his trip, entered just then, saw the glow on her face, and looked the inquiry he would not speak. But Sara understood the look.

"I have been much pleased," she explained, "by this." and handed him the enclosure.

"What! Really an article in the *Science Made Popular?* Well, Miss Olmstead, you are to be congratulated!" holding out his hand with great cordiality. "May I ask what you wrote about?"

She told him, and he nodded vigorously.

"Very good, very good! I shall watch for its appearance; and now I've a proposition to make you. Would you like to study Latin and French?"

"I?" gasped Sara.

"Yes; they are much needed in our work, as well as German and Greek; but there must be a beginning. I have all the books you will need, and will hear your Latin recitation every morning. It won't take long, and I'm sure Madame Grandet will help you with the French."

"But they're going away soon, are they not?"

"He is, but she has half decided to remain. It's so delightfully quiet here in summer, and only a short run to the seashore; besides, she likes her boarding-place."

Sara's eyes shone.

"I think every one is very good to me," she said softly.

"Heaven not only helps those who help themselves, but earth, too, Miss Olmstead; which is only another way of saying that real effort always brings appreciation. Now we'll take hold of that last case I sent, if you please. I'll bring your books this afternoon - or, no; better stop in and let Mrs. Macon give them to you; she always enjoys a visit, you know."

But pleasure and pain always keep as close together as light and shadow; and while everything seemed going so prosperously with Sara in the business of her life, there came a new worry at home. Baby was evidently ailing. Each morning it became harder to leave that supplicating little face, and she would turn back to reiterate cautions to Molly, who, being out of school now, saved the extra expense of the little nurse-girl. Even after she had actually torn herself away from the fretful baby voice begging pitifully, -

"No go, Wawa; 'tay baby!" she would stop below at Mrs. Hoffstott's door to beg, almost with tears, that she would look after things a little, and not let flighty Molly neglect the child; which the good woman was always ready to do. Those were anxious days, which even the madame's and Mrs. Macon's kindness could not wholly relieve.

And they were very kind. The latter often took the two children to drive, while the former brought baby dainties and toys to brighten his languid eyes.

A doctor was finally called, who said his ill feelings were entirely owing to his teeth, and left some mild powders for him to take. But there came a night when he was so feverish and flighty that Sara dared not leave him in the morning, so sent a note by Morton to the professor, stating the reason for her absence. The latter read it carefully, said a sympathizing word or two to the boy, who plainly showed his concern, then added kindly, -

"Tell her not to worry at all about the work till the little one is quite well enough to be left; there is nothing pressing just now; and supposing you stop at the house as you go by, and let Mrs. Macon read this note. She is fond of the child."

"Yes, sir," said Morton, and was about to start on his return, when the gentleman arrested him.

"Stay," he said, "what are you doing since school closed? Are you working at anything?"

"Not much, sir; I'm helping Mr. Hoffstott in the bakery, carrying home orders on his busy days: it doesn't take all my

Fannie E. Newberry

time though."

"I suppose you are used to the management of boats; you can row or sail one?"

"Oh, yes, sir!" his eyes lighting.

"Very well, I may have a proposition to make you soon, that's all. Be sure and stop at Mrs. Macon's."

Morton obeyed, but only to find her gone into the neighboring city on a shopping excursion, so hurried on to deliver his kindly message from the professor, wondering all the way what that wise gentleman could have meant by his remark about the boat.

But when he reached home all these thoughts fled; for he found Molly just descending the stairs, crying bitterly; and when he asked what was the matter she only gave her hands a desperate wring and sobbed, -

"Oh, the baby! the baby! Where does that doctor live, anyhow?"

Hurrying in he found Sara, her eyes wild with trouble, and Mrs. Hoffstott, fairly purple with consternation, both trying frantically to bring the child out of a spasm.

"Oh, run, run for the doctor, Morton!" cried his sister. "Baby's getting worse, I'm sure; and Molly doesn't know the way."

Morton did run, but alas! it was of no avail. The poor little fellow had one moment of consciousness, in which he feebly tried to pat Sara's colorless cheek and murmur, "Wawa deah!" then the beautiful eyes rolled back, set and glassy, the limp, dimpled hand dropped on his breast, and the sweet baby life was over.

Sara gave a heart-rending cry, which reached Morton and the

doctor, now hurrying up the stairs; and when they entered she was calling piteously upon the little one with every loving term her tongue was used to.

The doctor drew her gently away.

"He is gone," he said with solemn emphasis; "his sufferings are over! Madam," to Mrs. Hoffstott, "pray take her away for a time; her nerves are all unstrung."

That good woman led the half-fainting girl below, and at once despatched Grisel for Madame Grandet and the minister of the church the Olmsteads attended, who were shortly there, doing their best for the grief-stricken little household; while in the evening both Professor and Mrs. Macon came, the latter much grieved that she had been away when Morton called.

All was done that could be done; and Sara, even in her grief, which was for the time almost overwhelming, so deeply had this one of her cares and responsibilities taken a hold upon her nature, was surprised at the number of friends who seemed to have sprung up around them. She did not know that the story of her love and her struggles had passed from mouth to mouth, and that for the moment she was a heroine in their estimation. Nor did she know, till days later, that the lovely little blanket of white roses which wrapped the tiny white casket in its soft fragrance, was the gift of some of those very students who had brought the blushes to her cheek by their too pronounced admiration.

It softened her grief to find so much genuine friendliness and good-will in the hearts of even the strangers about her; and when she wailed for baby through the lonely nights, so sadly missing the clasp of his warm, soft arms about her neck, there was no bitterness mingled with her sorrow.

"He has gone to his mother," she wrote Miss Prue. "I sometimes think she must have longed for him even in heaven; and I hope she knows that, if I ever neglected him, it was only

Fannie E. Newberry

because I felt compelled."

To which the good spinster answered, - "You have never neglected him, Sara; to that I am ready to bear witness. If God has seemed to bereave you, it is because he sees it is best; meanwhile, take comfort in this: you have been tenderer than many mothers, and more patient than many sisters, to this dear little brother who loved you so well, so do not let self-reproach add to your sorrow."

The words were a comfort, as they were meant to be; for, with the girl's supreme conscientiousness, she had been torturing herself for fear she had not done all that was possible for her dear one; and, as Miss Prue's word had always been law with her, so now she let it heal this unnecessary smart.

CHAPTER XV

MORTON HAS A PICNIC

The professor was almost fatherly kind to her when she took her place again at the familiar desk; and, seeing how fragile and weary she looked, gave her but short, light tasks through those long, hot summer days.

Nothing was said about renewing the so soon interrupted lessons for several days, then Sara herself remarked half timidly, -

"I have begun my studies again, sir, it is so lonely, and there is so little to do at home," her voice faltering.

He gave her a pleased look.

"That is right; the best thing for you! Work, my child, is not a curse, but a blessing to sorrowful man. Study, - write too. I happen to know they are ready to accept another article from you in *Science Made Popular;* I am acquainted with its editor. Why don't you give him some more of your rambles?"

Her sad eyes brightened. After all, there was something within her which no grief, no bereavement, could entirely affect. "I will," she said; "I will pick myself up and begin over again."

"That's right. And try some walks here, Miss Olmstead; you'll find much of interest out on the old road leading west, for

Fannie E. Newberry

instance. You need more fresh air and exercise, I'm thinking."

Sara took his advice, with much benefit to her health, as well as gain to her information and purse; for she found that "knowledge is wealth" in more ways than one.

Morton had been such a good, helpful boy ever since their arrival in Dartmoor, that Sara was almost as glad as he when the professor's thought about the boat was finally unfolded, and proved to be a proposition that the lad should accompany him on a geological expedition down a certain river not far away.

He wanted Morton to help in managing the boat, as well as in foraging for extra game and provisions along the route, and watching the stores, while he studied, sought, and speculated over his stony treasures; for all of which the boy should receive a certain consideration in money, not to mention the fun.

"Just think, Sara, to be paid, actually *paid*, for having the biggest kind of a picnic," he cried rapturously. "Now, who cares for the Mary Jane?"

For the next two days all was hurry and confusion, as he and Molly ran errands, packed and planned, with Sara to advise and help; and the third saw the grand start.

As the river was at some distance, the first stage of the journey must be made by land (a great drawback in Morton's opinion, but still to be borne with patience because of what was to follow), so the boat was mounted on a cart, and packed full of the camping apparatus, amid which the professor and the boy sat in state, while a grinning Hibernian drove the mild animal in front.

The professor, with his glasses, his white helmet and tennis-shirt, and a butterfly-net hung over his shoulder, was quite Oriental and picturesque; while Morton, with a broad straw hat on his cleanly shaven head, and a blue blouse belted with leather, enjoyed the thought that he looked like a cowboy, and perhaps he did: I've seen cowboys who did not look half so well.

At any rate, he felt as free and joyous as one, and rode away with a ringing cheer, echoed shrilly by Molly, who was wild to go herself, and could only be appeased by the promise of a real picnic with the Hoffstotts in the near future.

"Oh, dear!" she said, on the verge of tears, as the long boat-cart swung out of sight around the corner, and was lost to view, "it's dreadful to think I've always got to be a girl, and I may have to live a hundred years."

"Well, my dear, console yourself, then," replied Sara, "for you won't be a girl even ten years longer."

"I won't?"

"No."

"Now, Sara Olmstead, how do you know that? Oh, yes, you're joking me, somehow; I can see by your eyes, for of course nobody knows when I'm going to stop living."

"How old are you, Molly?"

"Why, I'll be thirteen in eleven months."

"That is," with a laugh," you were twelve last month; now in ten years how old will you be?"

"Let's see," bringing her fingers into play, "aught's an aught, and two's two," marking that down with her index finger in her left palm, "then one and one is two, why, that's twenty-two, isn't it?"

"Really, Molly, I'm ashamed of you to be so slow in adding."

"Well, I never did like addition, it's substraction I'm so smart in."

"Yes, it must be *substraction*, I think," sarcastically.

"Yes, that's it," with entire oblivion of her sister's accent; "and now I begin to see, when I'm twenty-two I won't be a girl?"

"Hardly."

"Yes; but I'll be a woman, and that's worse, isn't it? Oh! there's Kathie, and she's got some cookies that are too dry to sell; I'm going to help her eat them," with which laudable purpose away she ran, to forget the limitations of her sex in an operation dear to both.

About a week later came this letter from Morton.

DEAR SARA AND MOLLY, - As I'm all alone, with nothing to do, and the gnats won't let me sleep, and I've got more than we need to eat, so it's no good to hunt or fish, I thought I'd start a letter, and when I get to a post-office again I'll mail it. To begin at the beginning, we launched the Bonny Doon about two o'clock, and at once set sail for the south (we really poled the boat along, for there wasn't a breath of wind, and it was hardly deep enough to keep her afloat; but it sounds better to say "set sail," you know), and were making about four knots an hour, when I saw the professor open a long wooden box I had noticed among the outfit, and take out a gun, all in sections, and begin to put it together. That made me feel better, for I was really afraid he had forgotten how useful a gun is out camping; and I was so taken up watching him fit it together that I almost forgot my poling, till he suddenly sung out, for all the world like a regular sailor, "Hard a-port, lad! Mind your course there, or we'll be swamped," and, sure enough, I had to swing her out into the stream, or we'd have run aground.

But that was the end of the marshes, and then we did rig up our sail, and 'twas a fine old fly, I tell you. My, how I enjoyed it! The breeze had come up a little, and sent us cutting through the water as slick as your big knife cuts through a loaf of bread. We didn't stop at all, till it was time to make camp, and then we had a real good time, for the professor is just like a boy here.

He cut saplings for tent-poles, and showed me how to make the pins, and fasten down the canvas, then we built a nice little fire, and put our camp-stove over it. It is nothing but a big piece of stove-pipe, I should think, with a griddle on top, but works first-rate; and then we got supper together. You ought to see his camp-chest, Sara! It isn't much bigger than that old desk Miss Prue gave you, but it has everything in it, I should think; and there isn't an inch of waste room. I found everything I needed to set the table with, and we had canned things, and biscuit and cheese and coffee, and lots of nice things to eat. Then I washed the dishes (I'm real glad now, that I learned at home, for the professor said I did it as neatly as a girl), and then he went off, poking around with his hammer, and I fished. You don't know much about fishing with a jack-light, do you? It's good fun. I caught enough for breakfast, nice little perch they were, and then we lay down on our blankets, stretched over pine-boughs in the tent, with mosquito-netting over all the openings, and slept like two tops.

Yesterday we had lots of adventures. First thing, I woke up just in time to save our provisions from some hogs which had smelled us out, and came down on us in a regular drove; and they got us so wide awake we concluded to stay up, though it wasn't really morning yet. But you don't know how good our fried fish did taste! I ate till I was ashamed, and then finished the bits in the spider; and I could have eaten as many more, I guess. Then I cleared everything up ready to break camp, while the professor went off again, and then he came back, and we embarked. This was about six bells, I think. We hadn't gone more

Fannie E. Newberry

than two knots when the boat began to slip along so easy and fast I couldn't understand it, till the professor sung out,

"We're coming to a dam! Put her about, quick!"

Then he grabbed the oars and rowed with all his might for shore. It seemed at first as if we would be swept along in spite of ourselves; but he's got more strength in his arms than I'd thought for, and then, luckily, a great tree had fallen clear out into the stream, which I reached for. I threw myself almost out of the boat, just holding by the toes, and caught hold of a little twig, then a stronger one, and pulled the boat an inch at a time till we were safe alongside in a perfect little haven. Then the professor dropped the oars, took off his helmet, and wiped his face, for he was dreadfully warm; but he only said, -

"That was a little close, Morton; now we'll have to make a portage."

Well, that wasn't so much fun. I hadn't thought, before, we had one thing more than we needed, but now it seemed as if we had a thousand. Sara, it took us four hours to make that portage, and my back hasn't got over aching yet!

We managed to get two men to help us with the boat, but that was only a small lift, it seemed to me; and I was glad enough when the professor said we'd take a rest before we went on. But the dinner braced us up a good deal; one thing we had was some roasted green corn one of the men told us to pick in his field, and it was awfully good, but not up to the fish. Then I stayed to watch camp while the professor went hunting for more stones and things, and then I had the biggest adventure of all. But I'll have to tell you about that in my next letter, if I come across any paper, for this is all I've got.

Yours truly,
Morton.

It came in due time, fortunately for Molly's welfare and Sara's comfort, as the child was so consumed with curiosity over the adventure that she gave her no rest from questions and conjectures. Here it is: -

DEAR SARA AND MOLLY, - I think I stopped because I was out of paper, and so didn't tell you about the tramps. There were three of them, and I never saw worse looking men.

I was sitting reading one of the books we brought, when I thought I heard something, and looked around just in time to see them come towards me out of the woods. I felt my heart leap right up, for I was all alone, and they did look wicked. The foremost man had a big stick for a cane, and both the others carried long switches they must have cut in the woods. As I jumped to my feet the first fellow said to sit still, sonny, he wasn't going to disturb anybody, and wanted to know where my pard was.

I said, as careless as I could, that he was just down below, hoping they'd think I meant down on the shore; but they didn't, for another spoke up and said he was far enough away, "and don't stop to palaver, I want some grub!" I'd kept backing towards the tent all the time we were talking; and when he said that, I was right in the opening, and one look inside showed me the gun almost where I could reach it, and I knew it was loaded!

I felt a good deal bolder then, so I told them, -

"You'll have to wait till the professor comes back; these are his things;" but the men only laughed in an awful fierce kind of way, and said they "guessed they didn't care about waiting, sonny, they wasn't making formal calls, and they hadn't brought their cards, but they'd leave suthin' to remember 'em by just the same!"

The way they talked fairly froze me up, though 'twas a real

Fannie E. Newberry

hot day. So I ducked inside and grabbed the gun, but they thought I was so scared I was trying to hide; so they went around kicking things over a good deal, and swearing like everything, but I didn't care, for there wasn't much outside the tent anyhow, except the cooking things and some mouldy bread that they were welcome to if they wanted it. When they saw how it was, one of them came up towards me, and called to the rest to come on, they'd have to explore the tent to find what they wanted.

I let him come to about two feet of the opening, then I stuck my gun in his face real quick, and yelled "Halt!" as loud as I could, and he halted.

I told him then he'd better get back, for this might go off, and he ripped out a big swear word, and told me to stop fooling with that gun or somebody'd get shot; and I said I was afraid they would! He kept backing all the time, and saying, "Oh, put it down, put it down, sonny!" but I kinder thought I wouldn't. Then they all stood off, and threw stones at me, and said they'd set fire to the tent, and for me to come out like a man, and they wouldn't hurt me; but I thought as I was just a boy I'd stay where I was. But I told 'em I'd shoot the first man that came near the tent, and their stones didn't amount to much anyhow, for they didn't reach me. But I really did not feel quite so saucy as I talked, for if they hadn't been regular cowards they could have made me lots of trouble, I guess; and when I saw the professor's big white helmet coming through the trees, I tell you I was glad! I called out, "Don't mind the men, sir, I've got 'em covered with the gun!" and at that they gave one look at him, and ran for the woods. He stood still and looked after them as surprised as anything; but when I told him all about it, he laughed and laughed in that still, funny way he has, and said he guessed he didn't make any mistake when he chose his companion; and I thought perhaps he meant to praise me, but I'm not sure. This is all about the tramps.

Good-by, Morton.

P.S. - I've torn my pants; but the professor says, "Never mind, there's more where they came from," and he looked at me kinder winkey when he said it, for you know they were made out of his old ones. This time it is really

Good-by, Morton.

Sara was so proud of these letters that she could not resist showing them to Madame Grandet and Mrs. Macon, both of whom were greatly amused.

"He has evidently gotten into Henry's good graces, as well as his old clothes!" laughed the latter. "The boy is like you, Sara, he doesn't know how brave he is."

Sara looked up quickly.

"Brave, I brave?" she asked in surprise. "I never did a really brave thing in my life!"

"Didn't you?" smiling, with a meaning look. "I thought you had done a good many."

But she made no explanation of her words, and Sara was too modest to ask what they meant.

Morton came home so brisk and rosy it was good to see him, and regaled Molly for days with the accounts of his wonderful adventures. He seemed to have quite recovered from his longings for a sea-life, and was almost as much interested in certain scientific studies as Sara herself. In fact, their autumn rambles together were pleasures whose memory lingered with both for many a year.

One morning in November, Sara saw, among the letters on the desk, a creamy square with her own name upon it, and nearly had her breath taken away upon opening it, to find it was an invitation to a dinner given by one of the faculty in honor of a distinguished scientist from abroad, who was to deliver a lecture before the students the coming week.

She glanced from it to Professor Macon, who was busy writing, but, seeing no solution of the matter in his face, resolved to consult his wife about it, and stopped in on her way home that noon for the purpose. "Oh, you are invited, then!" cried Mrs. Macon with satisfaction, as Sara explained her errand. "I was sure you would be."

"But how could you think so? I, a fisherman's daughter."

"You, Sara Olmstead, the writer who is already being noticed in the literary world! Why shouldn't you be asked, I'd like to know?"

"But, dear Mrs. Macon, what shall I wear? how shall I act?"

"Ah! now you are talking sense. 'What shall you wear?' Sara, you must have a white dress; something with long, soft folds, and - yes - and trimmed with swan's-down. That will be so becoming."

"Yes, and cost a small fortune!"

"No, not as much as you think. A cashmere will do, and that reminds me, I'm to have a dressmaker here the first of the week; she shall give me an extra day or two, and make your dress, then I can be sure it is all right. And never mind about the swan's-down; for I have some on a dress, I think almost enough, that I have only worn once. She shall rip it off for you to wear on this great occasion."

"O Mrs. Macon, how good you are!"

"Good? Why, this is fun for me. You must go with us, of course. Yes, and we'll ask the Grandets to go in our carriage too; 'twill make five, but no matter; you're little, and can squeeze in between the two gentlemen for that short distance: and, fortunately, cashmere doesn't show mussing badly."

"But, Mrs. Macon, I'm afraid" -

She stopped, coloring daintily.

"Well, of what?"

"Won't you be - ashamed of me? I never went to a dinner-party in my life. There are a great many forks and spoons to manage, aren't there?"

"Simplest thing in the world, that, my dear; begin with whatever is next your plate. If you think you are wrong at any time, dally a little, and watch your hostess. By the way, this invitation is for two weeks ahead, and Thanksgiving is next week, Thursday; you shall practise here! I was going to see you soon, to invite all three of you to dine with us that day; will you come? We shall ask the Grandets also, but no one else."

"You are exceedingly kind, Mrs. Macon; we will be more than happy to come. I had dreaded the day," softly.

"Yes, my dear, anniversaries are sad things; but we will try and enjoy this one. And don't hesitate to ask about anything that puzzles you at our table. These little fads of etiquette are easily learned, after one has acquired that real politeness which must become a part of the character; and that you have, Sara."

"Thank you for your encouragement, dear Mrs. Macon; I shall try not to put you to the blush."

CHAPTER XVI

THE PRINCESS HOLDS A "DRAWING-ROOM"

When Morton heard of the two invitations, and something of the foregoing conversation, as they sat over their cosey supper that evening, he kept quite still, while Molly was running on with questions, suggestions, and comments, till there was a lull; then he looked up at his elder sister with a queer expression.

"Supposing, Sara, I had gone with Uncle Jabez Wanamead, and then should come home a rough fisherman, while you were learning how to be polite; would you have been ashamed of me?"

"No, Morton; but I shall be much prouder of you if you will have the bravery and honesty of a fisherman, with the education and manners of a gentleman, and the spirit of a Christian; that ought to make a man for any sister to be proud of."

"Well," he said, drawing in his breath, "I'll say it now, Sara, I'm glad you stuck out so against my going in the Mary Jane. While I was off with the professor we were by the sea a day or two, and I went aboard a smack. It was a better one than that, too; but I was glad I hadn't a berth there, for somehow things did look dreadfully rough to me that day. There was a boy about my age, and the men swore at him nearly every word they said, and he swore too, and chewed and smoked and drank his grog; and he seemed real proud to think he could take it down clear without staggering. I was glad to get back to the professor, Sara, but I *would* like to have a yacht of my own, and sail all over the world after specimens for the museum; wouldn't that be fine?"

"Perhaps you may some day; who knows? Stranger things than that have happened."

It was a very nice-looking trio which turned into Mrs. Macon's gate after church Thanksgiving Day. The checks Sara received for her articles were of great assistance in clothing them comfortably for the winter; and she glanced with almost motherly pride from tall Morton, in his neat overcoat and derby, to Molly, pretty as a pink, with her flying curls and scarlet cheeks, in a dark blue serge trimmed with fur.

She forgot herself, but no one else would have done so; for the slender figure in black, with a close-fitting jacket and trig little hat, was so symmetrical, while the face above had such a charm, both of feature and expression, that few could pass her by unnoted.

Mrs. Macon welcomed them with gay cordiality.

"Dear me! How sweet you do look, Sara!" giving her a motherly kiss. "But you'll have to look out for this young lady or she'll eclipse you yet!" pinching Molly's dimpled cheek. "How the child is shooting up! I've a surprise for you, Sara. I hope it will be a happy one."

"I think your surprises are always happy, Mrs. Macon."

"As are your remarks, Sara. Well, come, Madame Grandet is below."

They descended to the beautiful drawing-room, where, in the softened light, Sara was conscious of several figures; the madame, lovely in a Frenchy toilet, with a dash of scarlet here and there, rose to greet them, while the little group of black

Fannie E. Newberry

coats just beyond separated and turned, resolving itself into her host, Professor Grandet, and - Robert Glendenning!

The last named came forward with an eager movement, and Sara's heart stood still a minute, then plunged on with rapid beats, as he took her hand and bent over it with an earnest greeting. He looked well, as she quickly observed, having broadened into proportions better suited to his height, and his eyes seemed more brilliant than ever as they met her own.

"This is my surprise, Sara," laughed Mrs. Macon; "and you know," mischievously, "they are always happy ones. I think you have remarked it yourself."

But Sara only answered by a look: her words did not come readily just then.

"He have come last night," said the madame, beaming upon her nephew, "so that it was to all of us a surprise, for we have not expect him."

"Indeed! As if you could think, Aunt Felicie, that I would eat my Thanksgiving turkey in a boarding-house, when" -

"Ah! but that is what you would then do, if our friends had not so kindly invite us here, Robare; are not your uncle and myself also in a boarding-house?" a reply which rather non-plussed the young man for a moment.

But, fortunately for his embarrassment, the domestic just then announced dinner, and Mrs. Macon said, -

"Henry, will you give your arm to madame? And you, Mr. Glendenning, to Miss Olmstead; I will do myself the honor of walking in with Professor Grandet; and I'm sure Morton will be happy to escort his better half, as I suppose a twin sister may be called."

As they passed through the hall, Sara's escort said in a

low tone, -

"I have heard of your sorrows and your joys through my good aunt. Tell me one thing, is your life any happier, broader, better, amid these new surroundings?"

"Yes," said Sara, "I believe it is; and yet, sometimes my very soul is sick for the sight and sound of the sea, and for the roughest greeting from one of our good old weather-beaten fishermen at home."

"I am glad that is so. You are too loyal to forget easily; but still you would not go back, would you?"

"No, never;" smiling up into his face. "There is no plan for going back in my life; only for going forward."

He smiled in return, but the bustle of taking their seats prevented any answer. When all was quiet again, Sara had time to notice that she had been placed where she could observe every motion of her hostess, and even as the thought crossed her mind, she caught that lady's eye and a telegraphic glance passed between them. Sara's said, "Help me!" Mrs. Macon's replied, "Watch me!" at which both smiled slyly, and turned to the next neighbor with some light remark.

Morton and Molly had been so drilled in their deportment before they came, that each sat now stiff and solemn as martinets awaiting some command; Morton, eying hopelessly the tiny bouillon-cup before him, with the healthy appetite of a boy who had not eaten anything since an early breakfast; while Molly, after a stony rigidity of perhaps two minutes, suddenly gave a little twist and drew a sigh as long and lugubrious as the wail of an autumn blast. Professor Macon looked at her with twinkling eyes.

"Don't be discouraged, Miss Molly," he whispered leaning towards her, "there is a turkey somewhere, I'm sure, for I had a sniff of it myself some time ago." Her eyes brightened, and she whispered back in the same confidential way, -

"You see, I don't like beef-tea very well, and I do love turkey. But, of course, if it's the thing" - and she submissively took up her spoon, prepared to attack the decoction.

Sara's cheeks had grown red at this; but when the professor added, -

"Between you and me, Molly, I think it's only fit for sick folks myself; but I suppose, as the saying is, we must eat by the card;" at which everybody laughed good-naturedly, her worried feeling wore off, and she began to think it would not, perhaps, be an unforgivable offence if one of them did commit a blunder or two.

In fact, by the time the bouillon disappeared to make room for the next course, she had quite forgotten her worries, so deeply was she interested in what Robert was telling her of the wonderful growth and vigor of his city home, Chicago; while the children, unwatched and well occupied, fell into order like well-trained soldiers; Molly now and then flinging out some *naive* remark which sent a ripple of laughter around the table, at which Morton would begin trying to frown her down, in his elder-brotherly way, and end by laughing with the rest.

When the ladies had returned to the drawing-room and coffee, leaving the gentlemen deep in a political discussion in the professor's snuggery, just off the dining-room, Mrs. Macon saw the children happily interested in some beautiful photographs of European scenes, viewed through a powerfully mounted lens, then turned to the others.

"Come," she said, "I want you to go up-stairs with me, and see Sara's dress. My dressmaker has done wonders the past week, and it is nearly ready."

They followed her to the little sewing-room, which Sara so well remembered as the first apartment of this hospitable house into which she had ever been introduced, and there lay the white gown over a chair. After viewing it critically, Sara in a quiet rapture, and madame with all a French woman's enthusiasm and epithets, Mrs. Macon said impulsively, -

"Do try it on, Sara; I'm a little afraid about this skirt; it looks short in front, and you know she has had to go almost entirely by measure, so far; here, let me pin the rest of this swan's-down in place, while you take off your dress."

Sara obeyed without a murmur, feeling all the delight of any young girl in trying on her first evening gown, while her two tire-women stood by, patting, punching, pulling, and commenting, as women will, pronouncing it a perfect fit, and quite long enough. When it was finally adjusted, they stepped back, and the little madame drew a long breath.

"Ah! but she is beautiful!" she said in her own language; "she might be one of the old noblesse," while Mrs. Macon, controlling her delight, remarked, -

"It is becoming, my dear: you have one of those peculiar complexions dead white only enhances. You look taller, too, a full inch, in that train. Really, the children ought to see you; let's go down-stairs and take them by surprise."

Sara, believing them still alone, did not object; and Mrs. Macon, if she had heard a closing door, and steps through the hall below, did not think it necessary to mention the circumstance. So down they went, the two attendants in front, and Sara following, with possibly a little intensification of her usual measured and stately tread. Thus they entered the drawing-room, the two ladies parting to right and left before her, as might two maids of honor attending some royal personage, the stately white-robed figure advancing, with head slightly bent, as if in modest disclaiming of all this parade over one so young.

"Oh!" cried Molly shrilly, "it's Sara, and she looks like a

queen!" while the three gentlemen, farther down the room, turned quickly from their talk, and one said, under his breath,-

"A princess, indeed!"

Then they all surrounded her, even dignified Professor Macon showing his enjoyment of the masquerade, while Professor Grandet spread out both hands, and cried, "Beautifool! Beautifool!" in a French rapture.

Only Robert Glendenning said nothing more, unless eyes speak; but Sara did not seem to miss the lack of words on his part.

"It is strange, now," observed the host reflectively, after the first outburst had subsided, "what a transformation dress is! I shall never again quite dare to think of Miss Sara as a little girl; she has crossed the brook, she has entered into woman's kingdom, and all because of a long white gown!"

Sara turned to him.

"Oh, please, sir, I'd rather be the little girl. I" - with a pathetic tremble in her voice, "I'm barely twenty yet, and I've never had much of a girlhood."

The little cry, right from her heart, sent a thrill through every one; and there was not a person in the room, even to careless Molly, who did not, then and there, resolve that whatever was in their power should be done to bring that brightness into her life, in which it had been so greatly lacking. Robert Glendenning sought his aunt's eyes, and in his she saw an indomitable resolution, while in hers he read a sudden yielding, which made his heart leap with joy; for he knew no step could be a happy one for him which did not meet with her full approval.

The rest of the evening passed swiftly and merrily away, Sara once more in her plain black dress, modestly bearing her part in the bright, animated conversation, in which even the children were interested, as well as instructed. When they separated to their homes, Robert said, -

"Miss Sara, with your permission, I will walk home with you; I want to see where you live, and besides, there are a good many lawless students on the street to-night."

"And won't we see you again, Mr. Glendenning?" asked his hostess.

"I fear not, Mrs. Macon; I leave to-morrow at nine o'clock."

"Your stay is short."

"Yes, very; a business trip mostly, which I managed to bring about to take in Thanksgiving Day. Let me thank you for helping to make it one of the happiest I have ever known."

"I think," smiling mischievously, as she gave him her hand, "your thanks are due elsewhere; but as I never refuse anything that is offered me, so I won't these; and allow me to say," with intense meaning, "as far as I am concerned, you are *most welcome!*"

"Thank you again! Miss Olmstead, are you ready? I'll be home soon, aunt; good-night, Professor Macon," and Sara was conducted down the steps, her heart beating, and her head whirling with new, strange, unfathomable thoughts.

The dinner-party came off in due course of events, and Sara went through the ordeal with credit to her quartet of guardians. Indeed, she made so favorable an impression upon several that they really longed for a more extended acquaintance, and, for a time, invitations became quite a common affair. But she accepted these most sparingly.

"I can never return them," she said to Mrs. Macon, "and I do not like to be under obligations, except to those I love," with a sweet look into her friend's face.

Fannie E. Newberry

"Yes, my dear, that is right, only in these cases the people expect no return, knowing fully your circumstances; your acceptance and enjoyment repay them sufficiently."

But Sara shook her head. She had her own ideas of these things, and besides, it was no trial for her, the doing without society. Here, as in Killamet, she preferred books to people; though she was often charmed to find herself deeply interested in some individual, who upon acquaintance developed qualities she had only dreamed of before. But it was simply as individuals that these interested her; taken *en masse* the world of men and women seemed cold almost to cruelty. After one or two evenings out, she went back to her books with a warm feeling of attachment.

"You cannot disappoint me, dear old friends!" she whispered lovingly, and the next invitation was answered by a formal regret.

So the winter passed quietly and swiftly away; for busy time is always swift time, and all three of our Olmstead household were thoroughly busy: Sara with her writing added to the museum work; Morton with his studies, in which he was growing deeply interested; and Molly in a little of everything. She had no special fondness for books, but a real genius for cookery and housework, most of which now devolved upon her in their modest establishment. But Molly was growing very pretty too, not with Sara's delicate, *spirituelle* attractions, but with a saucy, piquant, bewitching charm of her own that the students were not slow to notice, and which Molly was not slow to appreciate, and make the most of.

Still, Sara did not for some time take any notice of this; for she could not understand that what to her was a nuisance, and to be gotten rid of at once, was to Molly the source of the greatest amusement and delight, - their street admiration and attentions. It came upon her with a shock, one day, to find herself on the sidewalk behind some tall-hatted young sprig, accompanied by her little sister, rattling on to him with smiles, dimples, and tosses, in her own peculiar way, as if she had known him all her life, and she could scarcely wait to get the child indoors, before she began, -

"Molly, who was that?"

"That? Why, I've forgotten his name," coolly. "He's a 'fresh' though, I believe."

"And you're one, too, I should think!" strongly indignant. "What in the world were you doing?"

"Oh, just talking and laughing."

"When you don't even know who he is? O Molly!"

"Well, what of it? All the girls talk to them, coming home from school, and nobody thinks anything of it but you!" pouting and frowning, in her growing anger.

Sara looked at her with suddenly-awakened eyes. Even in her petulance she was wonderfully pretty, with her great surprised eyes, saucy little nose, and exquisite coloring; and a sudden sense of her helplessness, if this little sister should also prove to be vain, and careless of her good name, came over her with such crushing force that she dropped into a chair, feeling almost faint for the moment. Molly, frightened at her sudden pallor, cried out, -

"What is it, Sara? What have I done? Is it such a sin to walk with a student on the street?"

Sara shook her head helplessly.

"If I could only make you understand, Molly: you *must* understand! See here," with intense earnestness, "we are all alone in the world, Molly, you and Morton and I, all alone, except for a few friends, whose only interest in us depends upon our worthiness. Don't you see how careful we must be?

We have no home, no money, no anything, except our good name: we must keep that! Nothing, nothing, must take it from us. The Bible says it is more precious than rubies, and it is, Molly, it is; indeed, with us it is everything! If you had a father and mother to back you, possibly you could make such acquaintances without harm, though it seems to me a hazardous thing, even then; but now it is absolutely dangerous! Promise me, Molly, that this shall end it."

"If I promise I shall break it," said the honest girl; "for they *will* speak to me, and I shall forget when I'm away from you."

"Then, Molly," with sudden resolution, "I shall resign my position, and take you back to Killamet. I can make enough with my pen to keep us from starving."

Molly looked at her, and knowing she was in deadly earnest burst out, -

"Oh, don't do that, Sara; 'twould be too dreadful! I'll try, I really will; but you must remember I'm not like you. I don't care for books, and I do like people; and it's awfully lonesome with nobody but you and Morton! Other girls have parties and rides, and lots of nice times; and I don't even have girlfriends to come and visit me; it's lonesome, it is!"

Sara felt the force of this as she had never felt it before. Here was a nature as opposite to her own as the two poles. The books, thoughts, and work, which gave her such pleasure were all a weariness to this sunny, companionable creature, longing for life, merriment, and all youthful pleasures. Could she greatly blame the child? And her tones softened as she said, -

"Poor little girl! Have I kept you too close? Believe me it was for your good."

At this Molly weakened instantly, and two arms flew about Sara's neck, while a penitent voice cried, -

"I know I'm just as mean as I can be, and you're the best sister in the world; but oh! I do wish I could ride horse-back, and go to parties and picnics, and have stacks of girls all the time, then those silly students might go to gr - I mean to College, where they belong; for I wouldn't care a cent for the whole lot of them!"

Sara laughed. After all, there was something in this honest, transparent child, from which evil had always seemed to slide, as dust slips from a polished mirror; and she said with conviction, -

"Molly, we'll both do differently. I like people too little, you perhaps too much; but after this I'll cultivate a fondness for them. There is no reason why we shouldn't both go out more, in certain ways, and see something of the life about us. If you will give up these wretched street acquaintances you shall have a party next Saturday."

"A party? O Sara!" her eyes dazzling in their delight.

"What kind of one?"

"A tea-party. Let's see, you might have nine girls, besides yourself; that would about fill our table, and I'll wait on you. I presume Morton will be off, as usual, on a geological ramble, so we needn't count him."

"O Sara! and may I have the table trimmed, and flowers all around? And may I make the cake? And oh!" clasping her hands together, "may I have Mr. Hoffstott freeze some cream?"

"Yes," laughed Sara; "yes, every one, if you'll keep your part of the contract."

"Sara," with intense solemnity, "if a student speaks to me I'll look right through him, like this," with a stare of Gorgonian stoniness; "and if he isn't completely silenced, I'll wither him this way," and she swept her sister with a slow, lofty,

Fannie E. Newberry

contemptuous glance, that would have scathed an agent.

"O Molly! Molly!" was all Sara said, as she laughed in spite of herself; but she felt she could trust the child who, with all her faults, had not a grain of slyness or deception in her nature.

CHAPTER XVII

MOLLY GIVES A PARTY

The party came off, "according to contract," as Molly observed, and for a few days kept the child in a flutter of delight. Sara purposely left the preparations to her, only giving advice as it was requested; and even she, though so well acquainted with Molly's housekeeping abilities, was astonished at the result. It gave her real respect for the girl to see the method with which she planned it all, from her list of invited guests to her list of grocer's stores, arranged with the probable cost at the side of each article, that Sara might understand just how much money would be needed.

Then the dishes she compounded, after intense calculations over the cook-book, and frequent racings down-stairs to consult with Mrs. Hoffstott, were really toothsome and delicate; besides being brought about with precision and forethought, so that all might not crowd together at the end.

"Now," she said, Friday night, consulting a much-worn bit of paper, and drawing a long, house-wifely sigh, "now I'm all ready, except the salad, and laying the table, and the decorating. If I only had a screen to put before the range, so that we needn't have the table in here! it will fill up so."

Sara looked up.

"There is one in our cloak-room at the museum. Perhaps the

Fannie E. Newberry

professor would let you take it for this grand occasion, if Morton will bring it home for you."

"Would you, Morton? would you?"

"Oh, I suppose so; anything for peace!" growled the latter, just glancing up from his Burroughs.

"That's a lovely boy! Well, and the flowers - how glad I am they're so cheap, now" -

"Oh, yes, Molly! I forgot to tell you: Mrs. Macon says she has a quantity of early blossoms in her hot-bed, and you can have a picking from them."

"Now, Sara, if you had forgotten that! How good she is! And I'm to have Mrs. Hoffstott's pretty old china, with the blue forget-me-nots, and - well, isn't everybody kind, anyhow?"

Sara put down her book with a laugh.

"Go on, dear; what's the use in trying to read when there's a party going on? Talk to me about it; I want to know all the arrangements;" and happy Molly ran on like a thoroughly well-oiled windmill for at least twenty minutes without a stop.

When, at the end of that time, there was a pause for breath, Sara said, -

"And how about the students?"

Molly gave a merry little laugh.

"It's the greatest fun, Sara! They can't understand at all; they look at me as if I was a Barnum's fat woman, or something, and I sail right by, with my head up, and never see them. I think" (reflectively), "if anything, it's better fun than the other way. That was too much like every girl you see, and this is just me alone: I really enjoy it."

"Molly, you are incorrigible!"

"What's that? I wish you wouldn't use such big words, Sara; I never could understand them; but if you mean I don't keep my promise, it isn't so! I do: you can ask Maud Wheeler if I don't."

"Is she coming to-morrow?"

"Yes; and she's your kind, Sara, - good, you know. You'll like her, and so do I, when I'm in my right moods, but sometimes I don't. You don't know, Sara," with a pathetic shake of her curls, "how hard it is to get along when you have bad streaks through you! Why, sometimes I'll go on for at least three days as smooth as can be, getting all my lessons, and being just as good as anybody; and then there comes a day that upsets it all. I can't study, and I see all the funny things, and how I can make 'em funnier with a touch; and I want to giggle at everything, and - well, it's that naughty streak, and I can't help myself, any more than you can help being good."

"Well, Molly," resignedly, "promise me this, that, whatever you do, you'll be out and out about it: no hiding, no shirking, no lies." "I never told a lie in my life, Sara Olmstead, never!" with a set of her bright head that was like the elder sister in her determined moods. "I'd feel mean forever!"

Sara smiled, and, with a rush of tenderness, bent forward and kissed her.

"No, darling, you won't lie, thank God! Now go to bed like a good girl, and be bright and rosy for to-morrow. Good-night!"

"Good-night, you blessed old sweet thing, you!" and with twenty kisses, and a strangling hug, the merry child ran off to dream, - not of students in elevated hats, but of creams and comfits, and pleased guests around a long table; for she was but a large-hearted, hospitable matron in embryo.

The party was really a brilliant success. Mrs. Macon sent a basketful of bright flowers, and some pretty draperies and decorations; while the professor willingly agreed to let the screen go, and insisted on Sara's taking the whole day off to assist at the *fete*. The madame came herself, and with deft fingers, and perfect taste, helped the two convert the little flat into a bower.

No one would have known the back room, with bright rugs covering its painted floor, and all the kitcheny suggestions hidden behind the ample screen; while the parlor was really charming in its tasteful dressings.

When the girls began to arrive, Sara watched her little sister with almost a dazed feeling. How rapidly this flower she had so cherished was unfolding before her eyes! And what was its quality to be? No modest daisy or violet certainly, nor yet a gaudy, flaunting tulip, but something bright, sweet, surprising, and enticing, all at once; and she thought of a carnation-pink shooting up from amid its ragged foliage, vivid, brilliant, and of a spicy fragrance. She watched the guests, also, with a critical eye, and was much pleased to note that Molly had shown good taste in their selection. They were all ladylike girls, evidently from good, well-guarded homes, and, though merry and care-free, had not a touch of vulgarity.

Madame Grandet had begged the privilege of remaining to help with the supper; and you may be sure every dish was served with a perfection and daintiness of touch only the French can give. Yes, it was a great success; and when, after the last guest had departed, Molly came and told her sister, almost with tears in her eyes, how happy she had been, Sara felt repaid for the sacrifice of quiet and seclusion she had made.

But she knew one party would not keep Molly. The active, restless, rapidly-unfolding nature must have constant occupations and interests; so for the sister's sake she did what she never would have done for her own.

She began to cultivate the social life of her church; went to Christian Endeavor meetings, socials, and Y.M.C.A. addresses. She made Morton go with them too, half dragging, half coaxing him; and soon the three, so dissimilar, yet all so intelligent and well-bred, came to be looked upon as most necessary factors in entertainments and social events.

When Sarah left Killamet, though she wore her white cross, she did not change her membership into any new circle of King's Daughters, but still remained one of Miss Prue's "Helpful Ten," as they called themselves in that little town. Now she and Molly joined a Dartmoor circle, and were soon known as active working members.

All this took time, thought, and money; and many times it was a puzzle to find the latter, though she had been drawing a slight advance in salary for several months, and Morton, by working in the college laboratory at odd hours, was now earning enough to clothe himself.

Yet, even with an occasional extra cheque for her published articles, the expenses were so increased that she often had difficulty to meet them; though, to Sara's great credit be it said, the girl had never allowed herself a useless debt. She dare not; the very thought frightened her, and Providence having blessed her with health, and simple wants, it had been possible to live within her income.

Summer advanced with her languid days, and the great event of the year in Dartmoor - class day - came and passed.

Last year her only interest in the parade had been that of a stranger seeing for the first time a novel spectacle; but this year things were different. She and Molly now knew many of the students; knew them in an orthodox, well-regulated manner, and met them in both private and church parlors. Morton sometimes brought them home at evening as well, and occasionally the girls went with one of them to a concert or lecture. Mrs. Macon often had the sisters to assist at her receptions, and occasional dinners also; and thus, without being society girls at all, in a certain sense they yet did see a good deal of the social life in Dartmoor in one way and another.

Professor and Madame Grandet meanwhile were far away, the former having joined a governmental party bound for South America, while the latter had gone to Chicago to be with her nephew during her husband's absence.

She and Sara had agreed to keep up an occasional correspondence; and it was impossible that these things could be kept out of the letters, when they occupied so much of her time and attention.

One evening the madame and Robert returned from a drive to Washington Park, by way of beautiful Michigan Avenue and Drexel Boulevard, and as they were re-entering their private sitting-room in the house where they boarded that lady espied a missive slipped into the edge of her door, and gave a little cry of pleasure as she tore off its end and drew forth the closely-written sheet.

Robert, too, knew the bold, graceful chirography, and watched her hungrily as she read.

"I should think," he said at last in an ill-used tone, "you might read it aloud. It isn't very comforting to try and guess at it second-hand from your face, if it is a speaking one!"

She looked up with a laugh.

"But thou art cross, then, my poor boy? Well, listen and I will read, though blame me not if it is not always so pleasant to hear.

"MY DEAR FRIEND, - Time slips by so rapidly in our busy life that I can hardly realize whence it has flown, or recall in just what manner the hours have been spent. I told you in my last about the Bazar, and that an organ-concert was in progress. I'm sure you'll be interested to know it was a success, and the necessary funds are now nearly raised. Molly gave a song, also a recitation, and I was so foolish as to consent to read an original sketch.

"You should have heard and seen Molly! I was surprised at her myself! Her singing is so easy and natural, and her manner so vivacious, that no one seems to notice that she hasn't any voice. At any rate, they recalled her twice, and it was then she gave the recital on, which is half a song, you know, of 'Christmas at the Quarters.'

"They fairly shook the house with applause then, but she would not go back again.

"No," she said to me in her frank way, "it's time for the other girls to show off now - I'm done."

"(I'm sure Molly will never be too highly cultivated to call a spade a spade!)

"Morton is developing a good voice, and sang in the choruses. I think I have spoken to you of the young man he meets so often in the laboratory, and so greatly admires, Mr. Preston Garth. He also sang that night - he has a magnificent baritone - and it was quite funny to hear his and Molly's sparring, when he went home with us afterwards.

"He tells her frankly that she has no method, no voice, no tone, etc., - I am not used to musical terms, - and she saucily replies by telling him that, where one person will enjoy his studied renderings of the old masters, a score will appreciate and be the happier for her little ballads, simply because she discards all methods and sings from the heart; and usually Molly talks him into silence, I suppose because he is too much of a gentleman to set her down as she deserves - the pert little Miss!

Fannie E. Newberry

"It is useless for me to interfere, however, as both insist on finishing the argument in their own way. Mrs. Smythe has a party tonight; you remember Mrs. Smythe's parties - 'a little gossip, less lemonade, and no cordiality' - to quote Mr. Garth" -

A sudden exclamation from Robert, as he sprang to his feet, interrupted the reading.

"What does that insufferable puppy mean? Who would ever have thought that Sara, little Princess Sara, would stoop to quote, and run around with, some fool of a singing student, an ill-natured one at that! I can't" -

"Robert," said his aunt severely, "how can I then read if you do thus make a jack-that-jumps of yourself? Can you not sit down once again while I continue?"

He sat down, frowning fiercely, and she read on, -

"'which is too severe, but made it easier for me to refuse his kind invitation to accompany me there. I often wish I could learn to like society better, if only for Molly's sake; but it is still too much in the way of a duty that I take what, to a well-regulated mind, should be a pleasure.'"

"Humph!" muttered the nephew, with a relieved look; and his aunt read the remaining page in peace.

It spoke of the Macons, her last article, etc., ending with the modest sentence, "and now, pray remember us all most kindly to your nephew."

Robert's face lighted up at this, though there was a lurking trouble in his eye. "Aunt Felicie," he said abruptly, "what am I waiting for?"

"How can I that thing tell, my nephew? Is it that you have need of me to mend a button, or" -

"Don't tease, auntie! You know I don't mean any such trivial thing. See here," fiercely, "it's been nearly three years, instead of one, and I've never changed, not for a minute. I've kept myself as pure and true as a man could; I've done everything you told me to; and now how do I know but some fellow, with a voice, has stepped in and spoiled it all! I say, what am I waiting for? I've a good salary."

"Good enough for four, Robert? If you do marry Sara, it must be to adopt the twins also."

"Well, I will! We can scrimp along somehow; and Morton will soon look after himself. I wish you were back at Dartmoor this minute so I could" -

"A thousand thanks, my boy, it is a truly kind and filial wish," said his aunt demurely.

"Aunt Felicie, you're enough to make a man wild! Why don't you help me out of this, instead of tormenting me so?"

"Ah, Robare, my too impatient one, could I then help you? No; if she loves you, then what is it to matter if there may be a hundred of fine young men about her now? And if she loves you not, then alas! could I create that love? Do not so foolish be, my son."

He felt the force of her remarks, but inwardly chafed at the way he seemed to be tied up here for the present, both by business and his aunt's presence. He dared not put his happiness to the test of a letter. That would seem abrupt and strange, with so little to lead up to it. No, he must do as he had been doing all along - just wait.

"But not for long!" he muttered, as he bade his aunt a preoccupied good-night and strode off to his room. "We'll 'bide a wee,' Sara, but only a wee, or my name is not Robert Glendenning!"

Fannie E. Newberry

CHAPTER XVIII

A VISIT FROM MISS PRUE

It was only a few days after sending this letter that Sara received a proposition from Mrs. Macon which she was not slow to accept; namely, that she should give up her room, store her furniture in the loft of their stable, and keep the Macon house for the summer, while its master and mistress took a long western trip. As they wished to retain their excellent cook as well as the gardener, these were to remain, at the Macons' expense, and assist in caring for the premises.

No need to say the Olmsteads were delighted with the plan, - especially as Sara had begun to feel that their rooms were far too close and stuffy to be healthy in warm weather, - so beautiful June had not yet begun to turn her back upon the young summer, when the Olmstead family found themselves lodged as they had never hoped to be; while the Macons, equally content with the arrangement, took their seats in a Pullman sleeper, unvexed by visions of tramps and fire, moths and carpet-bugs, or precious books ruined by dampness and mice.

The first morning after their arrival Sara woke early, wooed from her light slumbers by a charming bird-matinee in the shrubbery without, and gazed contentedly about her.

It was such a pretty bower. Clean India matting on the floor, and airy cane furniture, dressed up in pink and blue ribbons, scattered about; through the sheer muslin hangings at the windows the early sunshine glinted between the closed shutters, and danced in bars of light upon the delicately-tinted walls.

She nestled her head into the soft pillow with a sigh of intense satisfaction.

"One whole summer of luxury!" she mused. "Is it possible? How wonderfully good our Father has been to us! Friends, comfort, and a beautiful home," and with these serene thoughts, mingling with the Pareppian carols without, she again dropped into her "beauty sleep."

Nor did this content vanish with her second waking, but seemed to grow with every passing day; for, as once all things seemed going against them, now all were in their favor. Morton, who had for some time given desultory help in the college laboratory, was offered a permanent position there at a modest salary for next year, with limited hours, so that he might still keep on with recitations in school; and meanwhile was to act as clerk in a drug-store until the opening in September.

As for Molly, she was as happy as a bird in these pleasant surroundings, and danced about the house all day long; now concocting some delicate dish in the kitchen, under the supervision of Hetty, the cook, who had taken a great fancy to her; now taking an old dress or bonnet of Sara's, and, by a dexterous touch here, or a perked-up bow of fresh ribbon there, giving it an altogether new and elegant appearance; or else feeding the birds, or lounging in the hammock, chattering with a group of girls, - always busy, happy, and useful, if her studies were quite forgotten.

For Molly was as domestic as Sara was bookish, and relieved the latter now of so many little cares, that she found much more time to devote to her writing, especially as her duties at the museum were merely nominal during the professor's absence, chiefly attending to the specimens he occasionally sent on, and forwarding such of his correspondence as she was not empowered to dispose of herself.

To Sara the most attractive room in the house was the library, and she passed some of the happiest hours of her life in its quiet recesses. Here, every bit of wall-space, half way to the ceiling upon three sides, was given over to books; while the fourth, that opposite the door, contained a most artistic fireplace, above which, in lieu of the sometime mirror, the chimney had been divided to insert a window, one perfect sheet of plate glass, almost as clear as the ether itself through which was a delightful vista of green mingled with the vivid glow of blossoms.

The three other windows formed arched niches, apparently cut through the book-shelves; and in one was a comfortable knee-hole desk, containing all the paraphernalia of a literary worker; while in the others were the most seductive of reading-chairs, with book-rests attached.

She had been sitting one day, smiling and crying alternately over "Bleak House," when a sudden thought brought her to an upright position, - why not invite Miss Prue to visit her? When would she ever again be so fortunately situated to entertain her pleasantly?

"I'll do it at once!" she said, rising briskly; "Molly will be as delighted as I with the idea, for she has often wished Miss Prue could see how well off we are;" and not giving her resolution time to cool, she seated herself before the desk and wrote the invitation.

It was promptly accepted; and a week later Morton met at the station, and conveyed home, a rather old little figure, with the traditional band-box and bird-cage in hand.

"Here we are!" she cried merrily to the waiting girls on the piazza. "Both the spinsters, you see, for Polly and I are too old to be separated!" and, setting down the cage, she proceeded to embrace each pretty young creature with motherly warmth, Polly meanwhile remarking hoarsely, -

"How d'ye do? Go 'long! Come again! Oh, you fools!" at which Sam, the gardener, appeared wonderingly around the corner of the house.

"Beg parding, Miss," jerking off his ragged straw hat, "but I thought as how you might be havin' trouble with a tramp," glaring savagely at Miss Prue; "thought I heered a strange voice."

"Oh, it's nothing, Sam, nothing but a bird," laughed Molly.

"A burrd!" he cried, with an amazed look. "A burrd a-talkin' the likes o' thot? May all the saints defend us!"

While the laughing group stood by, Molly introduced the fowl, with proper explanations, at which Polly, probably thinking it necessary to vindicate her powers, broke out with, -

"Hold yer jaw! Get out! Shiver my timbers! What the" -

"You disgraceful old thing!" cried Miss Prue, snatching up the cage and rushing indoors, where she set it down with a thump on the hall-table; and, dragging off her black silk wrap, proceeded to muffle the profane creature in its shiny folds; then, turning to Sara with a distressed look, she implored, -

"*Will* you tell me what makes her so wicked? I've tried my best to teach her nice little moral axioms from Ben Franklin and Socrates, and bits of poetry from Tupper, but whenever she wants to show off, she goes back to that dreadful old sailor-talk she learned on shipboard, nobody knows how many years ago; it's discouraging!"

"It is, indeed!" laughed Sara, while Molly furtively lifted a corner of the wrap, in hopes to start Polly off again. "But never mind Polly's capers, dear Miss Prue, we know what a respectable old bird she is, in spite of her lapses. Come into the library, where it's nice and cool, and tell me everything you can think of about dear old Killamet. Oh, how good, how good, it is to see you again, you blessed woman!" throwing an arm about her, and hugging her up rapturously, as they passed into the opposite apartment.

"What a paradise!" cried the elder maiden, stopping short on the threshold. "Do you tell me that is a window, in the middle of the chimney, or only some wonderful picture? I didn't know a room could be made so beautiful, could express so perfectly the refinement of work" - then breaking loose from Sara's embrace, she faced the young girl, and, taking her by the shoulders, held her at arm's length, and gazed at her critically. "Let me look at you," she said, sweeping her glance slowly from the proud little head, with its earnest, refined face, down over the lissome figure in its sheer, white gown, even to the daintily-shod feet peeping from beneath it, "let me see whether this is the niche you were intended for. Yes," slowly and reverently, "yes, I see. You fit in here; you are content, satisfied. It isn't the luxury, either, Sara; that you could do without; it is that better part one can hardly name, only feel; and your Maker has been slow in shaping you that you might fit the more perfectly. Kiss me, dear, I am glad you are *my* daughter!"

Sara kissed her tenderly, her eyes wet with tears of happiness; and Molly and Morton entering just then, with questions as to where Polly should be suspended, turned the talk into lighter channels.

The latter soon found herself chained to a perch of Sam's contriving, out on the deep veranda, and for the rest of her stay had a string of admirers ranged along the sidewalk at nearly all hours of the day, bandying words with her ladyship. As for Sam, he furtively admired her as much as the street-boys, and would be seen to slap his thighs and double over with silent merriment, when she was a little more wicked than usual; not that Sam was an encourager of vice; by no means; but as he confided to Hetty, -

"It do beat all nater to see that pious old gurrl so fond of a haythen creetur that's enough to disgrace a pirate hisself; an' the quareness of it just gets me, it do."

As to the "pious old girl," (according to Sam's disrespectful characterization of Miss Prue) she had quite given up in despair.

"Really, Sara," she remarked with deep melancholy, "it must be the city atmosphere" (Dartmoor was a town of perhaps fifteen thousand inhabitants), "for, you know, she never was so perverse in Killamet. I'm afraid she'll disgrace us all!" Upon which Sara would comfort her by saying that, as most parrots were trained by rough people, nothing better could be expected, and she was sure nobody would blame them; while Molly, the naughty little elf, would shake her curls with a solemn air, and exclaim, -

"It's a mercy the students and faculty are mostly away, Miss Prue; I'm afraid she'd have to be expelled if college was in session, in consideration of the morals of the institution!"

But, in spite of Polly's harrowing performances, it was a delightful visit; yet, as often happens with delightful things, it brought to Sara a new worry and a great temptation. There were several of the young people present one evening; and Miss Prue, enjoying the moonlighted veranda and the music from the gas-lighted drawing-room, as well as anybody, watched the little by-plays with keen, interested eyes. Among the group was Mr. Preston Garth, a tall, shapely young fellow, whose face was redeemed from plainness by a pair of large intelligent gray eyes, and a ready smile, accented by the whitest of teeth.

Miss Prue was attracted by his looks; and, being a close observer, she soon noted that, though he talked about

Fannie E. Newberry

laboratory matters with Morton, and was ready to joke or sing with Molly and the two older young ladies present, yet every time Sara addressed him, he turned to answer with an eagerly respectful air, different from the rather careless manner usual with the others.

The next day, as she sat with her favorite in the cool library, Molly being away on an errand, she asked, apropos of nothing, -

"Who is that Mr. Garth, Sara?"

The young girl smiled.

"Just what you see, Miss Prue; a college student, and seemingly a fine young man."

"But where does he live?"

"I believe in Trenton."

"Know anything about his family?"

"No, except that there are not many of them, I believe. At any rate, he has no parents. He's helping himself through college partly, though I understand he has a small property; that's why he works in the laboratory."

"H'm," Miss Prue bent towards the light to pick up a dropped stitch in her knitting. "He looks like a fine fellow; does he come here often?"

"Yes, rather," Sara answered carelessly, just then engaged in digging about the roots of a palm in the window with one of her hairpins; "he likes to sing with Molly."

Miss Prue did not answer, except by an expressive little grunt, and then, apparently, changed the subject.

"Do you ever hear from Cousin Jane nowadays?" ("Cousin

Jane" was Mrs. Norris, Jasper's mother.)

"I haven't lately. She did write me a few times, and I answered; but the last letter came in cold weather, - I should say, before February." "Yes. Jasper has a schooner of his own now, did you know it?"

"No; has he? That's fine!"

"Yes; Jasper always was forehanded, and he has laid by quite a snug little sum; then of course his father helps him; you never hear from him?"

"No; that is, he did write a postscript in one of his mother's letters."

"Did you answer it?"

"Not directly. I expressed my thanks, etc., to Mrs. Norris when I next wrote."

Sara had resumed her chair and sewing; but at this she laid it in her lap, and looked curiously at her old friend, wondering what categorical fiend possessed her this morning. Miss Prue knitted two or three rounds in silence, then remarked, with elaborate carelessness, -

"You and Jasper have always been good friends?"

As she ended with the rising inflection, Sara answered, -

"Oh, yes, always," and picked up her sewing.

"I've about made up my mind," added Miss Prue, lowering her voice to a more confidential tone, "to make Jasper my heir. His mother has been for years my nearest of kin, and Jasper's a fine lad, honest and trustworthy. But I have some notions about woman's rights in property matters; and if I knew just the girl he would marry, I should leave it to both, share and

Fannie E. Newberry

share alike. I know whom he *wants* to marry," she finished decisively. "Is it Dolly Lee?" asked Sara, all interest.

"No, it isn't Dolly Lee," dryly; "it's Sara Olmstead."

The sewing dropped again.

"Miss Prue!"

"Well, it is, and you needn't speak as if I'd told a falsehood; for I *know!*"

Sara's cheeks had crimsoned warmly, and her voice faltered a little, as she asked, -

"Did he tell you himself?"

"Not in so many words; but I've known it, so has his mother, for a long time. He has cared for you ever since he was a little boy. And Sara," earnestly, "where would you find a better husband, a truer heart? I'm an old goose, I suppose, to speak out so plainly; but the fact is, Jasper's a bit afraid of you, and doesn't dare to speak, I imagine."

"Afraid of *me?*"

"Yes, he thinks you some kind of a goddess probably; most men do till they are married, and then they're too apt to think their wives are kitchen-maids; but I don't think Jasper'll be like that!" she added hastily.

Sara smiled.

"I've no doubt, Miss Prue, that Jasper would be all that is good and noble; ah! there is Molly coming back; I wonder if she succeeded in matching your yarn," and rising with a relieved air, she hurried out to meet her sister.

But the conversation lingered in her memory, and was often

brought to mind by trivial events. During all of her visit, Miss Prue had an air of taking possession of Sara, which was, if not new, at least accented greatly, and occasionally would drop such expressions as, -

"If you should ever live in Killamet again," or "When you come back to us, Sara," which gave the girl an uneasy feeling that her future was being settled for her, leaving no alternative. Even her very last day, during the packing, there was an instance of this.

Sara and Molly, revelling in the midst of bags and boxes, while pretending to help, came upon a little morocco case of antique appearance.

"May I look at this, Miss Prue?" cried Molly, holding it up.

"Of course, child; just hand me that bundle, Sara; it's bandages I brought along in case of accidents; I always carry some in my hand-bag, besides my old Indian ointment."

"Oh, how lovely!" exclaimed Molly, as the cover of the case flew back, discovering a set of coral ornaments of exquisite workmanship, outlined against the faded blue satin lining. "Coral's all out of style now, but it's wonderfully pretty, just the same; and what an odd design; see Sara!"

She held them out towards the latter, then by a sudden impulse took the ear-rings and placed them against her sister's shell-like ears.

"Oh! look Miss Prue. Aren't they becoming?" "Exceedingly," said that lady, looking around with a critical air: "coral always becomes such a complexion and hair. I've always intended those for Jasper's wife."

Her accent and tone were so peculiar as she said this that even Molly noticed it.

Fannie E. Newberry

"Jap's wife?" she cried gayly. "There's your chance, Sara. Why don't you set your cap for him, and the corals?"

"Molly!"

Sara drew back her head sharply, and thrust the jewels from her, but her face crimsoned as she did so; and though Molly dared say nothing further, her eyes danced with teasing merriment, while Miss Prue, pretending not to notice at all, took in every detail.

"Either she likes him so much she can't bear to have the subject made light of, or else the whole thing is distasteful to her; I wish I knew which it is," was her thought as she bustled about, apparently intent only on getting as many garments as possible into a given space.

She ruminated all the way home next day, making up her mind that she would not be quite happy now until this affair was arranged, and resolved that if Jasper happened to be at home when she reached there, she would have a word to say to him.

Meanwhile, Sara's tranquillity, having been invaded by this new idea, was effectually destroyed. It had been her life-long habit to reverence and obey Miss Prue; if she went against her in this matter it would be an unprecedented event. Then she could not but realize what a fine match it would be in a worldly point of view, allying her with those families she had, all her life, been taught to consider as first in her little world. It would give her dear ones certain comfort and herself rest from care and anxiety; she knew well what a warm nest Jasper's wife would step into, admired, petted, and cousined by relatives innumerable. Last of all, it would ally her to a young man she had always liked, and could thoroughly respect as well; one too, who would, she felt certain, be a tender, loyal mate. What was there against it? Why - as Molly would say - didn't she "jump at the chance"?

She felt really indignant at herself for her own perverseness; but, though she would not tell herself the reason why, she felt this thing to be impossible.

Better struggle along under her burdens as she had been doing, rather than go so reluctantly to that true and tender heart.

"Oh, I wish she had not spoken!" she whispered to herself passionately one day as these thoughts kept tormenting her. "I never knew Miss Prue to do so unkind a thing before! But why do I think about it? It's time enough to worry when Jasper speaks. Perhaps she's mistaken after all!" and she tried to content herself in this belief.

When a letter came from her old friend, giving a lively description of her journey home, and of a disgraceful squabble between Polly and a tiny pug, in which the former blasphemed, and the latter barked bravely from the arms of his mistress, until the wrathful conductor bundled both off into the baggage-car, but saying nothing of Jasper, except a casual remark that his schooner was expected in soon, she felt relieved.

"I have been making too much of nothing!" she said, and blushed all to herself at the thought that her vanity alone had caused her all these pangs.

Fannie E. Newberry

CHAPTER XIX

BERTHA GILLETTE

There was a great deal of sickness that summer in Dartmoor, and much suffering among the poor. Sara, having little or no money to spare, felt she could only give herself, and thus set apart her Saturday afternoons (upon which she was now free from museum work) to visit the sick whenever she was needed, the circle to which she belonged having systematized this charity that it might not fall too heavily upon any one.

Molly sometimes went with her, and the two bright faces brought comfort to many forlorn hearts.

It was an intensely warm day, the first week in July, when a card bearing the silver cross reached her.

"Bad case in third ward. A young girl in the Trask tenement-house, cor. G and Tenth streets. Can you go? Get whatever you need at Reed's, and ask for Bertha Gillette, third floor."

She turned to Molly.

"Is it to-day you have an engagement with the dressmaker?"

"Yes, at three; why?"

Sara read the card, adding, -

"I suppose I'll have to go alone, then. If I should be kept till dark, be sure and have Morton come after me."

"What makes you go, Sara? It's fairly scorching outside!"

"I know, but I must, you see. 'A young girl.' Poor thing! She may have no friends, and be suffering for care. Yes, I must go. I'll wear my thinnest muslin, and take the large umbrella."

She was soon off, stepping briskly in spite of the heat. The air was scintillating under the almost vertical rays of the sun, whose intensity was merciless, and scarcely a leaf stirred; even the birds were drowsy, and kept in shelter, while every house was closed and barricaded against the heat as against an invading army.

For a time Sara had the shade of the great trees lining the sidewalks for protection; but as she left these wide avenues for the alleys of poverty, there was nothing but her umbrella between her and the scorching luminary, while mingled with the intensified heat were the dust and odors arising from unsprinkled and garbage-strewn streets.

She felt faint before she reached the tenement-house, and only the consciousness that she must not give way to illness in this neighborhood gave her strength to proceed.

Once inside, she dropped down on the lowest step of the stairway, regardless of dust, until she had recovered somewhat, then wearily climbed the steps. Half-way up she met a rough-looking man, who scowled at her, but said nothing; and she hurried by him, glad to see he kept on his way without looking back.

Reaching the third floor finally, she saw a rather pretty little girl standing in one of the many open doors, and asked which led to Miss Bertha Gillette's room.

"She ain't got no room," said the child shrilly; "she's in old

Fannie E. Newberry

Mis' Pierce's room, down thar," pointing to a closed door; "that's whar they took her when they brung her in. There wan't no room anywheres else."

"Oh! Was she taken ill on the street?"

The child nodded.

"Got a sunstroke, I guess," and Sara hurried on to the designated door.

She knocked lightly, then opened it and entered. It was a bare little room, with one window, but decently clean, and the sash was entirely removed, being replaced by a mosquito-netting tacked to the frame, so the air was not foul. On the old bed in the corner lay the young girl, white and still, and beside her sat an elderly woman with a kind, weather-beaten visage, who looked up inquiringly.

"I am Sara Olmstead, a King's daughter," touching the cross on her breast; "can I do anything for you?"

"I'm glad you've come," said the woman; "I've did what I could, but I've got to go to my work now. I'm meat cook in a restaurant, and I must git there by four; it's 'most that now; can you stay?"

"Yes," said Sara. "Please tell me all about her, the symptoms, and so on. Was it a sunstroke?"

"Might be - set down, Miss, you look tuckered out yourself," handing the one splint-bottomed rocker. "I don't know much more'n you. They picked her up down on the corner this morning and brought her into the hall, - thought 'twas a fit, I guess. I come in while they was all tearin' around like a passel of geese, and when they didn't seem any place for her lower down, told 'em they might bring her to my room. I'm about the only one that rooms alone, I guess."

"And hasn't she spoken at all?"

"Yes, she come to and told us her name, but that's about all. She grew flighty pretty soon; and now she either lies still and breathes hard, like you see her now, or mutters suthin', I can't make out what. If you need any help, Mis' Maloney's a good, kind woman, three doors to the left; she'll come in a minute, 'less the old man's drunk and she has to stay to watch the children; and here's her medicines. I got the health doctor right away, Dr. Browne. Was it him sent you?"

"I presume he reported the case to our circle, and they sent me word. You said a spoonful every half hour?"

"Yes; and if she gets so't she really senses things, she might want suthin' to eat. You'll find tea and bread in this cupboard, see? and I bile the water on this oil stove."

Sarah nodded wearily; she was feeling a strange lassitude from which it was difficult to rouse herself. The woman noticed her pallor.

"You don't look strong yourself, Miss, and I hate to leave you, but I guess there won't be much to do. If we don't have a big run at the restaurant, - and we won't, it's so hot - I'll git back by seven sure; and don't mind calling on Mis' Maloney, she's as clever as the day is long. Well, good-by to you," and she was gone.

Sarah looked about her with some curiosity, noting the bare edges of the floor around the faded strip of cheap carpeting in the centre, the little stand with a white towel over the top, upon which was a lamp and a Bible, - she was glad to see the Bible - the woodcuts from illustrated journals tacked to the walls, and the one straggling geranium in a tin can on the window sill, then examined more closely the girl on the bed.

She was extremely pale, and there were blue shadows about her nose and temples; but the brows were delicately pencilled, the

Fannie E. Newberry

lashes lying against the colorless cheek, thick and long, while the hair, of a brown so light as to be almost yellow, curled naturally around her forehead.

"She is really pretty," thought Sara, "but how thin and blue. And what mere claws her hands are!" looking at the one clutching a corner of the sheet. "Poor girl! I don't believe she is much older than I, but she looks as if she had suffered enough for an old woman. Ah! she's speaking."

The lips were moving, but at first no sound came from them; then she caught one word, "mother," and then a tear rolled from the closed eyes over the white cheeks.

Sara gently wiped it away, thinking pitifully, "Where can her mother be?" and while the thought was impressed upon her face in a look of tenderness and pity, the eyes of the young girl opened wide and gazed into her own.

"Who are - you?" she asked faintly. "An angel?"

Sara smiled.

"No, only a girl like yourself."

"Then I am - not dead?"

"No, indeed: you have been ill, but are better now. Here is something for you to take," placing a spoon to her lips.

The invalid swallowed the liquid docilely, never taking her large hazel eyes from Sara's face.

"Who are you? Where am I?" she asked again.

"I am Sara Olmstead, a King's daughter, come to stay with you this afternoon; and you are in a good woman's room, who is now gone to her work."

The eyes closed again, and an expression of pain or regret passed over the face.

"Do you suffer?" asked Sara gently.

The head was shaken slightly.

"Not in body, but I'm almost sorry it wasn't true."

"What, Bertha?"

"My first thought, that it was all over, and you were the angel appointed to waken me in the other world."

The tone, weak almost to whispering, was infinitely sad, and Sarah thrilled with sympathy. That one so young should long for death seemed incredible to her hardy nature. But nothing more was said till, bethinking herself, Sara asked, -

"Could you eat anything now?"

The eyes opened quickly.

"Yes," she said eagerly, "yes."

Sara hurried to light the little stove and make the tea, managing also to brown a slice of bread over the flame. She looked for milk and butter, but found none.

"There is only sugar for your tea," she began.

"Never mind," said the eager voice again, "let me have it. Oh, how good it smells!"

Sara brought the plain little repast to the bedside, and, rising to her elbow, the young girl partook with an eagerness that was pitiful.

"Poor thing!" thought Sara, "I do believe she was starved!"

Fannie E. Newberry

then aloud, "If you can hold the cup, I'll make you some more toast; shall I?"

"Yes, please!" in a stronger voice, "I never tasted anything so good!"

While she was eating the second piece, Sara took a pencil and small notebook from her satin bag and scribbling a line, stepped hastily down the hall to the third door. It was opened by the same little girl who had first directed her.

"Is this Mrs. Maloney's room?" asked Sara.

"Yes'm."

"And you are her little girl?"

"Yes'm."

"Could I get you to do an errand for me?"

"Mebbe."

"It's to take this paper to Reed's store on G Street, and bring home the things the clerk will give you. If you will I'll give you an orange when you come back."

The child's eyes brightened.

"I'll go," she said. "Ma's down-stairs, and I'm minding the baby, but I'll call her."

"Thank you," said Sara, and ran back to her charge.

She was glad to see that the pale face on the pillow did not look so deathly now, and the blue shadows had nearly disappeared. She even smiled with some brightness, and her grateful eyes followed Sara about the room. A breeze had arisen, and was blowing refreshingly through the window, and the latter gladly seated herself where she could catch it all.

"You look better," she remarked, as she returned the sick girl's smile; "tell me, Bertha, was it from hunger that you fainted? I am your friend and want to help you."

"Yes, it was. I haven't eaten since - what day is this?"

"Saturday; it is now about five o'clock."

"Then it was yesterday morning. I had a piece of bread about as large as my palm."

"And nothing since?"

"Not a crumb."

Sara shuddered.

"Poor, poor girl! How did you come to such want?" tears of pity filling her sweet eyes.

Bertha gazed at her wonderingly.

"How did you know me?" she asked. "What makes you care?"

"I know your name because you gave it when you first came out of your faint, and how could I help caring? You are pretty near my own age, I think."

"I'm twenty-two."

"Then you are a little the older. Bertha, have you a mother?"

She shook her head sadly.

"No, I haven't anybody; it would have been better, I say. What can a girl do all alone in this great, wicked world?"

"Tell me about it, Bertha; perhaps I can help you."

No one could resist that tone; and Bertha, after one long look into the sympathetic face, drew a sigh and began.

"We were always poor, but not to real want. Father had a small farm, and we lived off from it till he died. Then it all went for debts and funeral expenses, and we took what little was left, mother and I, and came here. We managed to live while she was alive. She took in sewing, and I worked in Ball's factory, and we were as cosey as could be in our one room; but last winter she died."

Her eyes filled with tears, and she stopped a moment, then went on.

"The factory turned off a third of its hands in May, and I with them. I've tried everything since, but I'm not strong enough for many kinds of work. If I could only stand housework I could find plenty to do, but the heavy part is too much for me; twice I've broken down, lost my place, and had to use all the wages I'd saved up for doctor's bills. A second girl's work I could do, but it's difficult to get into those aristocratic houses, unless you have friends and recommends, especially in summer, when so many are closed while the families are away.

"I've done shop-work, and indeed a little of everything; but for a week I haven't had a thing, and I was reduced to my last crumb. I knew, if I couldn't pay for my room to-night, I'd be turned into the street, so for two days I've walked and walked, hunting for work, till I actually dropped, as you see. There's one thing, though," with sudden fire, "I've kept straight! If I had been really dead, as I for a moment thought, I would not have been afraid to meet my mother. But it's been a hard struggle! Do you wonder I was sorry when I found you weren't a real angel, and heaven was still far away?"

Sara, her eyes filled with tears, was about to answer, when Nora Maloney appeared at the door with her bundles.

"I've got 'em, mum!" she cried, and at sight of her bright face both girls smiled again.

"That's my good girl!" was Sara's approving comment; "and here, didn't I promise you something?"

"Yes'm," her eyes snapping, "an orange."

Sara opened a package, and took out two.

"What will you do with this, if I'll give it to you?" pointing to the extra one.

"I'll hide 'em both till pa gets away, an' then I'll divvy up with Nan and Jack, and Ma and baby," was the ready answer.

Sara handed over the two yellow globes.

"That's right! I'm glad you're such a generous little girl, and I am much obliged to you for doing the errand. Good-by."

"Good-by'm; thankee mum!" was Nora's hearty answer, as she hurried home to show her treasures, before it should be necessary to hide them from the father whom drink had transformed into a brute; to be avoided if possible, and if not, to be fed and cajoled, then, if still implacable, fled from in terror as from any other ferocious, untamable beast.

Sara took from the bundles oranges, grapes, biscuit, and sliced ham, the sick girl watching her, meanwhile, with eyes that grew brighter every moment.

"Now we'll have supper together," said Sara, arranging them neatly on the little stand; "for I'm getting hungry too, and while we're eating, we'll talk things over. That tea and toast will do for first course, try this bunch of grapes and the sandwich I am fixing for the second."

Bertha took them with a delighted air.

Fannie E. Newberry

"Oh, how good! We used to have grapes at home; and father always cured his own hams. I was never really hungry in my life till nowadays. We've always been poor, and sometimes I didn't have any best dress, but there was never any lack of food. Do you know" - solemnly - "it's an awful thing to get so hungry? I could have stolen - murdered almost - for food, only I didn't dare touch anything for fear of jail. All my ideas of right and wrong were confused, and for the time I was more of a wild beast than any thing else - oh, it was dreadful!"

Sara gently touched the thin hand.

"Poor girl!" she murmured, "I know something of it too!" then aloud, "Bertha, how would the place of a companion suit you?"

"A companion?"

"Yes, to an invalid lady. I know of a Mrs. Searle who needs one. She is rich, and ought to pay well; but she would want somebody who could read intelligibly - and I suspect it would require infinite patience to put up with her whims."

"I haven't a bad temper," said Bertha simply; "and I used to read aloud to mother while she was sewing - we both of us liked books. How I wish she would try me!"

"Perhaps she will; at any rate, you shall be looked after in some way. I am poor, myself, but I'm sure our circle will see that you find work. Do you know what the 'King's Daughters' are?"

"I've heard of them, but you're the first I ever met. If they're all like you, the Lord must be proud to own them."

The sincere, almost childish, tone in which these words were said divested them of any irreverence. Sara merely smiled, as she told Bertha some of their aims and practices; and when Mrs. Pierce returned, she was astonished to see her patient sitting up in bed, with almost a flush on her cheeks, and a glad light in her eyes.

"Lawful suz!" she cried in the doorway, "what have you done to her?"

"Fed her," laughed Sara; "and I have been helping her to take my prescriptions, you see. Won't you join us?"

"Well, I'm beat! Thank you - guess I will. Was that all't ailded her - jest hunger?"

"That's all," answered Bertha for herself, "and quite enough too!"

Then she repeated something of her story, thanking the good woman heartily for her kindness. It was decided she should stay till Monday with Mrs. Pierce, who seemed anxious to befriend the girl, though so poor herself; and Sara finally left them, still planning most amicably, in order to reach home before darkness should necessitate Morton's coming after her.

"How much cooler it seems!" she thought, as she stepped into the street, glancing up at the sky, which was partially overcast with purplish-black clouds; "I wish, now, I had brought a wrap."

She hurried on; but the storm moved more rapidly than she, and just as she turned into the avenue she felt the splash of a large raindrop in her face. She attempted to raise her umbrella, but a sudden squall of wind nearly wrenched it from her grasp, and, becoming convinced it would be impossible to hold it against the now shrieking blast, she made no more effort to raise it, but ran on - the rain falling more heavily every moment.

By the time she sprang up the steps into the shelter of the veranda, she was thoroughly drenched. Morton met her there, just about to go in search of her, with a waterproof and overshoes, and cried, -

"Why, Sara, how wet you are!"

"Yes," she shivered, "I'm drenched," and hurried on and up to
her room without more words.

By the time she was disrobed, however, that same sensation, as
of utter weariness, came over her, and she concluded to retire
for the night, telling Molly - who soon came up - that she was
tired and thought she had better get some rest.

"I've been to supper," she added; "and Molly, tell Morton
when he goes to the store, to-night, that I'd like him to do an
errand at Mrs. Searle's for me, on the way. Just hand me a
sheet of paper and a pen, dear."

"Won't it do in the morning, Sara? You look so tired!"

"No, to-morrow's Sunday, you know, and this is something
that must be attended to before anything happens."

She took the writing materials from Molly, and wrote the
explanation and request in regard to Bertha, then folding it
with a listless gesture, handed it to her sister.

"Don't let him forget - it's important," she said wearily.
"Molly, I'm *so* cold, can't I have another blanket?"

Molly brought it and ran down with the note.

"Don't stay late, Morton," she urged in a worried tone; "if Sara
ever was sick, I should say she was going to be now."

CHAPTER XX

WEAKNESS

Molly was confirmed in her surmise; for in an hour Sara was in a burning fever, and there was little sleep in the house that night. To have *Sara* ill was unprecedented - almost unbearable - and the whole household was visibly affected by it. Morton's face settled into a gravity which nothing could move, and Molly's dimpled visage had never looked so long and care-full.

Hetty bustled up and down, important and anxious, while Sam stood about in the hall, and asked everybody who passed along "how she wor a-doin' now."

The doctor came, looked wise, talked about malaria, exposure to the heat and over-fatigue, left some pills and powders, and went away again - after which the house settled down to that alert silence, so different from the restful quiet of an ordinary night. Sara, tossing to and fro in the fiery grasp of fever, moaned and talked, Hetty and Molly watching alternately beside her, while Morton tried to sleep in the next room, only to start from frightful dreams to the more harrowing reality that his beloved sister was actually and painfully ill.

It was a sharp illness, but not of long duration. The fever was broken up on the fourteenth day, but it left a very weak and ghostly Sara to struggle back to health once more. Still, there were no relapses, thanks to good care, for Hetty had been faithfulness itself, while Molly had settled down to her new

　　　　　　　Fannie E. Newberry

duties with a steadiness no one would have expected. As for Morton, he would have brought up half the drugstore, if he had been permitted, and was made perfectly content whenever allowed to share the night-watches, which was seldom, as he had to work all day. In these Hetty was soon relieved by those members of the circle who had become personal friends of the girls; and as there was little to do, except give the medicines regularly, they thus managed well without calling in a regular nurse.

Three weeks from the day of her seizure Sara began to sit up in bed, looking once more something like the girl of old, though she still talked (to quote Molly) as if she had hot pebbles in her mouth, and the veins on her temples were much too clearly defined beneath the white skin.

Thus sitting, one delightful day, she read a note from Bertha, which had been awaiting her some time. It was a rapturous expression of thanks for the good place she had found with Mrs. Searle, and begged that she might see her as soon as Sara was able. Molly said, as she handed it, "She has been here two or three times, begging to do anything for you that was needed, and I promised you should see her just as soon as possible."

So, a day or two later, Bertha came. Sara would hardly have known her, and indeed the two seemed to have changed places, - Sara was the weakling now, Bertha the strong and rosy one.

"I have such a good place," she said, in answer to the former's questions; "Mrs. Searle is very kind to me. Of course she is exacting and fretful at times, but that is only because of her illness, and I can get along with it; but she has given me a pretty room, and allows me an hour or two for air and exercise every day. I am happier there than I have been since mother died."

"That is good!" said Sara.

"And only think," continued the pleased girl, "she is talking now of going to the seashore. You don't know how I long for a sight of the ocean! The only trouble is, she can't find a place quiet enough to suit her - she hates to go to a great hotel, or where there is a crowd."

Sara looked up with a sudden thought.

"Killamet would be quiet enough - how nice it would be if she'd take my house there!"

"Your house! Have you a house?"

"Yes, the children and I; it's not much of one - just a cottage, but perfectly comfortable in summer. If Mrs. Searle would send down some furniture, I think she could really make it cosey."

"I'll tell her about it" said Bertha, and did, with the result that the lady decided to take it for the next two months, at a fair rental.

This little excitement over, Sara had only herself and the children to think of, and in her weak physical condition these thoughts were far from pleasant.

What was to prevent Bertha's experience from becoming her own, or possibly Molly's, in case of evil fortune? If she should often be ill, who would care for them? She seemed to herself, just then, such a frail plank between them and want! She raised her white, blue-veined hands and looked at them; they did not seem made for struggling, and a sense of powerlessness, born of bodily weakness, enwrapped her in its hopeless gloom.

There is a certain period, after convalescence is well progressed, that is even more trying to many natures than actual illness - that time when we are supposed to be well, and yet have not quite resumed our wonted strength.

Fannie E. Newberry

How the long-dropped burdens of our lives loom up before us now! Is it possible we ever bent our backs to such a load? Can we ever do it again? Yet, even as we hesitate, relentless necessity pushes us on, and bids us hoist the burden.

Sara felt this often now, and all her former bravery seemed gone with her strength. She had already decided that, next Monday, she must return to the museum, and bring up her neglected work; then there was a half-written article to be finished and copied, whose motive and central thought she had almost forgotten, while at her side loomed a basketful of stockings to be darned, and garments to be mended before the Sabbath dawn.

In this reluctant mood, trying to rally her forces for renewed conflict with life's hard duties, she could not help thinking how different it might all be - how she might be cared for, instead of looking out for others; how she might be the centre of a home, enclosed and guarded, rather than, as now, trying vainly to encompass one, making a wall of her feeble self to shelter others - and hot tears of rebellious weakness filled her eyes, and dropped slowly upon the trembling little hands, which were painfully weaving the threads to and fro through a preposterous hole in one of Morton's socks.

A step in the hall made her hasten to dash away the tell-tale drops, as Hetty knocked, before peeping in to say, -

"There's a gentleman in the parlor asking to see you, Miss Olmstead."

"A gentleman? One of the professors?"

"I don't think it is; I never see him before - it's a young man."

Sara rose, adjusted her dress a little, and descended to the drawing-room. In its close-shuttered condition she did not at first recognize the figure which rose to meet her, but a second look wrung from her almost a cry.

"Jasper?" "Yes, Sairay, it's me. You - you've been sick, I hear."

She bowed her head, unable to speak for the second.

"And you show it too," with an awed look into her lovely face, spiritualized by illness, as he took her extended hand.

"Yes," recovering herself, "but I'm nearly well now - how are they all in Killamet?"

"Oh, so-so, I guess; but I haven't been home to stay any since last month - soon after Cousin Prue was here, it was. I had business in Norcross yesterday, and I come over from there by train. Mother wrote about your having the fever."

She had motioned him to a chair, and dropped into another herself, feeling weak in body, and perplexed in mind. Why had he come? Was *he* the answer to her repining thoughts? His voice roused her from the sort of lethargic state into which she had dropped for a moment.

"Sairay," he said, with a little choke, "I - I couldn't stay away any longer - when I heard about you - and I've come" -

He stopped again, but she did not help him out - she could not. With her fingers locked together in her lap, she waited for what was coming, with the feeling that she was drifting down stream, and had neither the strength, nor inclination, to arrest her swift descent. He drew a sigh that was almost a gasp, and plunged on, -

"Sairay, it's too hard for you - all - all this - and I - Oh! you know how I love you - I've always loved you, and what is the use in your working so when I'd give my very eyes to take care of you? Don't speak, Sairay," raising his hand in protest, "I've got a-going, now, and I want to say it all. I know I'm not good enough for you - who is? - but if love that never tires, and kindness, and - and - being as true as steel, and as tender as a mother, can count for anything, they'll plead for me, Sairay;

Fannie E. Newberry

I'm not much on fine speech-making, as you know."

He had risen, and stood before her, tall and stalwart, and, for the moment, such strength and tenderness seemed good to her - why not accept them, and be at rest? Perhaps he felt her yielding mood; at any rate, he held out both hands with an assured gesture.

"Say yes, Sairay - tell me you" -

There was a jarring slam and a flood of light; one of the shutters had blown open. Both started, glanced around, then faced each other again; but that noisy interruption had thoroughly aroused Sara. She looked at Jasper in this brighter light, and a quick revulsion of feeling swept over her. What was she doing? Would she lie to him?

She did not love him; did she dare to tell him that she did? A thought of another manly figure, bearing a certain refinement and nobility lacking in this, rose before her mind's eye, and when Jasper finished his sentence - "tell me you love me!" her answer was ready.

"I can't, Jasper," she said low, but firmly, "It wouldn't be" -

He stopped her again.

"Don't answer me now; take time to think - take till tomorrow. This is too sudden; nobody can know their minds all in a minute. I'll come again when you've had time to think."

She shook her head.

"No, Jasper, that is not necessary. You have always been one of my best friends - be so still! But - that is all. I can't give you what you ask for, and time will never change me - don't think it. The best way is to have perfect truth between us. Now, Jasper," trying to speak easily, "put this aside, and stay with us this evening. I want you to see Morton and" -

"I can't," said Jasper, in a voice of intense calmness (she could imagine him giving an order in just that tone, when life or death hung on the proper execution of it), "I - must go. You - you're sure you know your mind?"

"Yes, sure."

He picked up his hat, - she noticed it was a silk tile, and thought vaguely how incongruous it looked upon him, though she was used to little else among the students, - and jammed it absently down on his head, as he was accustomed to fasten on his tarpaulin during a storm.

"Good-by" he said hoarsely, turning towards the door.

She stepped towards him.

"Jasper, wait!"

He obeyed - but reluctantly.

"I beg of you, don't let this make you feel hard towards us all. I have depended on your goodness all my life - don't let it fail me now!"

She held out her hand with that look which few could resist, a look of winning trustfulness words cannot describe. Jasper hesitated, turned, looked into her face - and yielded.

"Sairay," he said, grasping her hand closely, "it's no use; you always did have your way, and you always will! I'll be anything to you that you want me to be, but - it's bitter hard luck!" and, wringing her hand till it ached, he left her.

CHAPTER XXI

THE PRINCE COMETH

"A letter from Mrs. Macon, I think," said Morton, handing it across the table to Sara, with a glance at the western postmark.

"I shouldn't wonder if it is to announce their return," she remarked, opening it.

"Heaven forbid!" groaned Molly. "I love the Macons, but I adore their home! Why don't you praise these muffins, Morton? I made 'em."

"Is that what ails them?" making a wry face. "Give me another at once. We must make way with them as fast as possible!" and Molly passed him the plate, with a well-pleased laugh.

"Yes," interrupted Sara, looking up, "they will be at home inside of a fortnight, but she kindly says, -

"'Don't hurry to find rooms. I want to help you decide, and I shall be so glad to come home to a houseful of young people rather than to the usual gloom and stuffiness of long-closed rooms; besides, I have a proposition to make you.'"

"What can it be?" cried Molly. "She may want me to stay, in place of Hetty, for cook." "And me for coachman," added Morton, buttering his third muffin.

"Then, Sara, there is nothing left for you but to be lady's maid!" giggled the other twin.

"I should rather like the position," smiled Sara, "to read aloud to her, answer her notes, do her errands, and" -

"Button her boots!" put in atrocious Molly again, at which Morton slapped at her with his napkin, when she fled - pursued by him - to the veranda, where decency demanded a cessation of hostilities.

Sara soon joined them, and a little later, Preston Garth, - who was back in town for a day or so, to assist in setting up some new apparatus lately arrived at the laboratory, - strolled up the walk.

"You're too late!" exclaimed Molly saucily, as he dropped upon the upper step, and began fanning himself vigorously with his hat; "Morton's eaten up all the muffins, and I think Sara finished the peaches."

"And I suppose, as usual, Miss Molly had nothing," was the ironic reply.

"Oh, a trifle - not worth mentioning" -

"Yes, Molly has a starved appearance, as you may have observed," put in Sara. "But, Mr. Garth, in spite of her discouraging remarks, I think we could find" -

"Oh, thank you, Miss Olmstead - I have been to tea; just left the table, in fact, and am on my way back to the museum, so dropped in here. Has anybody noticed the sunset to-night?" All turned to observe it (the house fronted towards the south), and simultaneously exclaimed at its grandeur. The sun was just dropping behind a thunderous bank of clouds, closely resembling a range of mountains capped with snow, now tinged ruddily with the dying light, and between these crowding peaks was an arched opening, as if a vaulted passageway had been blasted through the mass of rock, giving a vista of pale blue sky, from which radiated prismic bars of light, while way above the topmost peak, like some beacon-light suspended high, swung the new moon, a slender crescent, also near its setting.

"Oh, I saw it over my right shoulder!" cried Molly gayly. "Don't you long to hear what wish I made?"

"Not half so much as you long to tell it," replied Morton cruelly.

"How snubbed I feel!" she sniffed, amid the laughter, making a face at him. "But if you knew it included you - Mr. Garth, do you believe in omens?"

"Really, Miss Molly, I never thought - in fact, I don't know of any, do I? What omens?"

"Oh, that you're going to quarrel, if you spill the salt, and that it's bad luck to step over a crack in the floor, and you musn't begin things on Friday, and" -

"Molly, what nonsense! I thought we agreed to forget all that kind of thing when the mirror broke," said Morton.

"Yes; when instead of bringing us misfortune it brought us comfort. Did we ever tell you about that, Mr. Garth?" asked Sara; then, as he gave a negative sign, she repeated the story.

He listened interestedly.

"Where did you live, then, Miss Olmstead?"

"In Killamet - a tiny fishing-village on the coast. We are the children of a fisherman, perhaps you know."

"You?" surprisedly. "I would never have thought it! I supposed" - He stopped in some confusion, and colored.

"Say it out!" urged Morton.

"Yes, relieve your mind," added Molly; "it won't stand too much pressure."

"Molly, be quiet!" interposed Sara peremptorily.

"Well," said the young man at this, giving Molly a queer glance, "I had always supposed fishermen to be a rude sort of people - entirely unlike you all, of course."

"'With the exception of one,' you would say, if you dared," added Molly instantly. "But you needn't blame any of my ancestors for my tongue - Sara will tell you our mother was a real lady, in speech and manners, and our father one of Nature's noblemen. I was probably changed in the cradle by some wicked fairy."

"Let us thank the creature for leaving such a unique specimen, at least," laughed Mr. Garth, completely mollified; (if you will not accuse us of an insane desire to make a pun). "Come, fairy changeling, and let's have a song together."

"Yes, if you won't insist upon classical music more than half the time. Do you know what I'd like to sing to-night?" rising to go indoors; "one of those rollicking, rioting old sailor-songs, with no tune, and not many more words, but with a catchiness in the two or three bars that gives you the sensation of a ship rolling and pitching under your feet - but Sara won't let me, so" - laughing mischievously - "I suppose I'll have to come down to Bach and Wagner!"

Sara left alone outside, for Morton now departed for the store, seated herself in one of the piazza-chairs to listen at her leisure. The twilight was deepening into the warm, scented dusk of a mid-summer eve, with nameless soft noises amid the dew and the perfume, as countless tiny creatures settled themselves to repose or came out for their nightly dance beneath the stars.

Fannie E. Newberry

The tender influences of night and silence inwrapped the girl as if in motherly arms, and she felt glad, and hushed, and still. What was the little struggle of a day when all this great, yet minute world lived, slept, woke and worked, subject to one Will - a Will mighty enough to control the universe, precise enough to make perfect and beautiful the down upon the wing of an insect invisible except under a powerful microscope? Why should she fret, or worry, or dread?

"I have but one care," she said, "to do right - to abide by my inner heaven-given instinct, which we call conscience, the rest is of the Will."

She leaned her head back restfully against the small down pillow tied by gay ribbons to her chair; but her resting soul leaned against an Arm, - mighty to save, and tender to feel. Amid all her musings ran the sweet strains of the old English ballad the others were singing inside, whose refrain only was clear to her, -

"Trust me, Love, only Trust!"

A figure moving with a springing motion came swiftly up the gravelled walk and mounted the steps. Not till then did Sara notice it. She turned, rose, and stepped forward; and as the figure advanced to meet her, it stood full in the light streaming through the drawing-room windows.

"Robert?" she questioned, still in a dream, and not realizing that she had used a name only whispered in her own heart till now.

"Yes, Sara," was the reply, "I have come - were you waiting for me?"

Still only half herself, so sudden and surprising was all this, she answered in his own tone, quiet, but threaded with deep meaning, -

"Yes, I - think I was."

He drew her to him, whispered three little words - and the new moon, just dipping her last upturned horn beneath the horizon, may have seen their kiss of betrothal; but if so, she modestly withdrew from sight, and never told the sweet secret.

I suppose my story should properly end here, but Sara felt that hers was just beginning. With arm linked in arm the two went softly down the steps, and strolled through the odorous hush of the garden, trying to tell the emotions of three years in as many minutes, while the unconscious couple within sang, and sparred, and sang again, perfectly certain of their unseen listener outside. After the first few moments, in which they could think of nothing but their own two selves, so strangely and quickly bound into one, Sara asked, -

"But how did you happen to be here just now, Robert?"

"Because I came! I was like a chained beast all the time you were ill, though Molly's letters gave only the most cheering news, but I knew I couldn't see you if I were here, and I mustn't leave aunt; but when word came from uncle that he was down with a malarial attack at Omaha, on his way home, and she started at once to nurse him, I made up my mind very shortly as to my next move - which was to pack my grip and come on, to 'put my courage to the test, to win or lose it all.'"

"It required a great deal of courage!" laughed Sara.

"More than you think, sweetheart. I was not at all sure of your feelings towards me - to tell the truth, I have been horribly jealous of that singing-fellow - what's his name - Garth, isn't it?"

Sara laughed merrily, and just then a booming strain rolled out from the drawing-room upon the silent air.

"Listen!" she said; "isn't that a fine baritone? That's something

Fannie E. Newberry

from Offenbach, I think."

"Magnificent!" returned Robert unsuspiciously, thrilling at her light, trustful touch upon his arm. "Who is it? Some friend of the Macons?"

"No, of ours. It is - Mr. Preston Garth."

He started, looked at her, and even in the dusk caught the amused flash of her eye.

"The rascal! Must I then run upon him the very first minute of my meeting you?" he queried tragically.

"Not necessarily - still perhaps, just for politeness' sake, we had better go back and say good-night to him. I think they have finished now, the music seems to have ceased."

They turned back towards the house just as Molly, who, with Mr. Garth, had now come out upon the veranda, cried excitedly,

"Why, she's gone. Sara! Sara! Where are you?"

"I am here, Molly," advancing with her companion, "here with - Mr. Glendenning."

"Oh!" said Molly; and Mr. Garth, feeling a sudden twinge of doubt and dread, waited but a moment longer, going through with the introductions almost mechanically - then, becoming suddenly aware of his neglected engagement at the museum, hastened on his way - leaving Robert in full possession of the field.

After answering a question of Molly's he entered the house with the two girls. They had just stepped into the brightly-lighted drawing-room, when the younger, a trifle in advance, turned with some light remark, and was at once arrested by the beatified expression upon both faces.

Her remark died on her lips; and her eyes, filled with wonderment, travelled from one countenance to the other, as if determined to drag the secret from them by mesmeric force.

"Tell her, Robert," said Sara softly; upon which Molly's hands came together sharply, after an old, childish trick of hers.

"No need! No need!" she cried with her usual frankness; "I'm not blind - and I never saw a couple so plainly ticketed 'sold' before!" Then holding out a hand to each of the somewhat abashed pair, she cried merrily, "It's lovely, though! And remember, Mr. Glendenning, I always share in all Sara's good things, so now you'll have to be my brother, if you have determined to be her - master," pointed by one of her indescribable grimaces.

"Master, eh?" queried the young man, raising his eyebrows. "Do you know, Molly, I shall be more than happy to be just her - husband?"

"Well, what's the difference? 'A rose by any other name,' you know; only look out for Sara! I never saw a girl quite like her; while she's seeming to give up she always gets her way" -

"As she has now!" put in that maiden with a happy laugh. "Don't tell Robert all my faults tonight, dear; let him have a surprise now and then."

"That means she is convinced that now you think her perfect," interrupted the saucy girl, with a trill of laughter. Then growing suddenly as gentle and tender as she had been elfish before, she added sweetly, "And Robert, you are right; you have won a real treasure - a perfect darling - as nobody knows better than her naughty, teasing sister."

Robert stayed a week, which time was to both lovers like a leaf blown back from Eden. The weather, as if in chime with their mood, was simply exquisite; and after the more imperative duties at the museum were over, they passed the hours together, walking, riding, or boating on the river, as utterly self-centred, and as foolishly happy as if one were not a thorough-going business man, and the other a studious worker and writer, beginning to make a reputation for herself. Just then the world, with its cares, its ambitions, and demands, was quite shut out, while love and happiness reigned supreme.

Such days, however, soon come to an end in this work-a-day world. An imperative telegram recalled Robert to Chicago and business; but not till he had won a definite promise from Sara that the marriage should take place the following October.

"So soon!" she cried, when he made the proposition. "But have you stopped to think? There is Molly - yes, and Morton, for I could not leave him here alone, though he is almost self-supporting now."

"Yes, I have thought it all out. My salary is not large for an expensive city, like Chicago, but we can all live upon it modestly, even there; and fortunately we none of us have extravagant tastes."

Sara's eyes filled.

"Robert, how good you are! Would you really burden yourself with my brother and sister? It is too much to ask!"

"I shall not look upon it as a burden, dearest. If they are yours they are also mine; and, as you say, Morton will soon take care of himself, for I can easily secure him a position there. As for Molly, we'll send her to school a while yet; but mark me, Sara, she'll be carried off before we know it, such a pretty girl as she."

"Well, there's one thing, Robert, I can write: you won't object to that?"

"Object! I'm proud of it! Write all you like, and be as learned as you please. The world may know you as a sage and a philosopher; but I, - ah! how little they guess what you are to me, my little princess by the sea! And now, if all your objections have been properly overruled, will you give me the answer I desire?"

"Yes," said Sara, "if" -

"There! You have said all that is required," laying his finger on her lips, "don't spoil it with conjunctions. A simple affirmative is quite enough; I'll imagine the rest," and Sara, only too happy to be thus overmastered, attempted no more objections to demands so sweet.

*   *   *   *   *

From this dream of bliss Sara plunged directly into a deep vortex of house-cleaning, for she was determined that the premises should be in perfect order upon the Macons' arrival. For four days chaos reigned, with the broom and scrubbing-brush for prime ministers. Morton took refuge at the store, but poor Sam, not so fortunate, had to face it all; and he felt as if the deluge had come again, with some new and harrowing accompaniments, in which woman's rights and demands were prominent. Then, on the fifth, they rested from their labors in the clean, soap-charged atmosphere - walking gingerly over spick and span carpets, laying each book and paper demurely in place, and gazing, at a proper distance, through diamond-bright windows; and on the sixth the Macons arrived.

They seemed delighted to be at home once more, and both looked unusually well, having gained in flesh and color. The professor was genial and serene, Mrs. Macon full of life and sparkle. She ran from room to room, like a child; then through the gardens and shrubberies, returning quite out of breath.

"O Henry!" she cried, "isn't it nice to find everything in such good condition? I remember after our last long trip it was really dreadful for a week or two - everything yellow and musty; mice and cockroaches camping in the library and

Fannie E. Newberry

bedrooms, and spiders everywhere. By the way, Sara, have you had to fight moths much?"

"Yes, occasionally. Molly has made a raid on them every week or so, with gasoline, I believe - I don't think they've made much headway."

"Well, it's perfectly charming; and I should break out into 'Home, sweet Home,' or something else equally original, if I had an atom of a voice. Now tell me all the news, - who's married, and to whom have the storks brought the blessed babies?"

"Yes, don't forget the babies," laughed her husband. "Marian has spent most of her trip acting as nursemaid to poor little sticky-faced souls, whose mothers were utterly discouraged, I'm daily expecting that the Society for the Prevention of Cruelty to Children will send her a gold medal, for I am sure she richly deserves it."

"Well, I shall be far more proud of it than of any old fossilized remnant of antediluvial times, I can assure you," was the quick retort. "And Henry needn't say anything, either, for he walked the coach-aisle a good half-hour with a crying baby yesterday - to be sure it had a lovely little mamma, who hadn't an idea how to manage it."

"Yes, it was all for the mamma," assented the professor demurely, with a twinkle at Molly, who was heartily enjoying the scene, and only impatient to put in her oar, as now.

"Did you have many engaged couples on the train?" she questioned wickedly. "I think they're worse than babies - so uninteresting, you know, besides being oblivious to the point of idiotcy. I've been *so* tired picking up after - oh! I nearly forgot myself - I mean generally speaking, of course."

Sara's face was a study, but one easy to decipher; for the cheeks crimsoned with embarrassment, the lips quivering with indignation, and the eyes aglow with a happiness no mortification could conceal, told all her secret in living characters. Mrs. Macon nearly sprang from her chair.

"*Who* is it, Sara? Mr. Garth - Mr. Steene - that little professor of mathematics with the bald head, or - oh! tell me, *is* it Mr. Glendenning?"

"What a wonderful guesser you are!" cried Molly.

"And not born in Yankeedom, either!" laughed the professor, really pitying Sara's distress.

Morton came to the rescue, as usual.

"If it is Mr. Glendenning, that's no reason for blazening it around all over the country, as if you were too proud of it to keep still. Robert Glendenning's a nice fellow, but I never saw anybody quite good enough for Sara."

"Nor I," said Molly, entirely unruffled; "but she's like those of royal blood, you see - she makes a man honorable by marrying him."

Amid the laughter over the cool impudence of this assumption, Sara recovered herself somewhat, and received with tranquillity the hearty congratulations which followed.

"I'm not a bit surprised - I saw it as long ago as last Thanksgiving," observed Mrs. Macon.

"Yes," put in her husband placidly, "Mrs. Macon's foresight is almost up to the Irishman's."

"Well, you may laugh, but I did - and what's more, I gave my consent. I told him he was *most welcome*, and he understood me!"

"That was generous," said the professor ironically, beginning

Fannie E. Newberry

to cut the leaves of half a dozen periodicals which awaited him upon the library table; at which the rest - taking the hint - adjourned to the veranda, to talk it over at their leisure.

CHAPTER XXII

GOOD-BY TO KILLAMET

The next day, as Mrs. Macon and Sara found themselves alone in the former's special boudoir, that lady remarked, -

"You haven't asked me yet what the proposition is that I mentioned in my letter."

"No," answered Sara with a smile, remembering their conversation over it; "are you ready to make it now?"

"Yes, and more hopeful of the answer I desire since I have heard of your approaching marriage. Sara, Henry and I want to adopt Molly."

"Adopt Molly?" repeated the sister, with wide, astonished eyes.

"Yes; she is just what we both need to give us an interest in life, and to make our home the bright, joyous place we want it to be. My original proposition was to have been that, while we legally adopted her, and gave her our name in addition to her own, so that there need never be any trouble about property matters, you should still keep up all your ties of kindred, and that Morton and yourself should find board near by, and make our house your second home. Then Henry would of course use all his influence to advance you both. Your marriage will change the plan a trifle, leaving Morton, as it does, somewhat unprovided for, and Henry has commissioned me to say that,

Fannie E. Newberry

if you will consent to our adoption of Molly, Morton shall have a home here, also, till of age, and all the help we can give him - though we will not adopt him as our own. What do you think of it?"

"I am so surprised, dazed, I can't think; it is most generous!"

"Not generous; we expect to receive all that we give; yet we won't be selfish, either. I don't ask you to give Molly up at all, in one sense - only to let us share with you in her love, and take from you all expense and care."

"Dear Mrs. Macon, you are a mother to us now - have been from the first day I saw you - and Molly is a happy girl to have won your approbation! She shall decide this matter for herself; I will consent to whatever she wishes."

"Then will you tell her, Sara? I want her to decide unbiassed by my presence;" to which Sara readily agreed.

But when told, Molly was even more amazed than her sister had been, and at first ran and clung to her, like a child about to be torn from its mother's arms.

The almost involuntary action touched Sara deeply, and for a moment the sisters remained locked in a close embrace, each sobbing uncontrollably. After a little they grew more quiet, and talked the matter over in all its bearings, and Sara could see that the idea pleased the child.

"If it was to give you and Morton up, I'd never consent," she said decidedly, "but it isn't. Mrs. Macon is just as fond of you as of me, Sara, and all the difference is that now you and Robert can marry without worrying over my future."

"We have never worried, dear; lay that up to Robert's credit, and remember that his offer of a home to you and Morton was as hearty and sincere as Mrs. Macon's own. I should not have been so fond and proud of him otherwise."

Molly, sitting affectionately on her sister's knee, toyed with her hair a moment, then said diffidently, -

"Sara."

"Well, Molly?"

"Don't be provoked, dear, but I've sometimes thought you would marry Jasper."

"Why, child?" trying not to color beneath the searching young eyes.

"Oh, he always seemed to like you so well; and Miss Prue too, I think she wanted it anyhow."

Sara hesitated a moment, then said gently, -

"I should consider it a great compliment if Miss Prue had felt so - and that makes me think - I must not delay longer to write her of these new plans of ours. And now, dear little sister, go to Mrs. Macon yourself, and tell her your decision. She is waiting in her own room."

"But you'll come with me, Sara?"

"No, child, best go alone."

"But what shall I say?" diffidently.

"Now, Molly, as if you were ever at a loss."

"But I so often say the wrong thing, and you never do, Sara," with a sudden spasm of feeling that brought hot tears to her eyes; "it doesn't seem right! You've been so good, and look at all the hard times you've had, while I'm just *penetrated* with naughtiness, and yet things always go smoothly with me!"

"Well, dear, then you have only to be thankful, and as good as possible; nor worry about me, God has blessed me abundantly."

A little later, Mrs. Macon moving restlessly about her pleasant room, heard a timid knock at the door, most unlike Molly's usual frank and earnest rapping; and at her invitation to enter, there appeared a much disguised edition of that damsel; for in place of the merry, fearless creature we all know, here stood a timid, blushing girl, apparently afraid to take another step forward.

Mrs. Macon felt inclined to a burst of laughter, which verged closely upon tears, as Molly sidled in, and began in a voice as soft as Sara's own, -

"Dear Mrs. Macon, I've come to be your child, if you want me, and it's easy to say I shall love you well, but" - suddenly breaking out into her usual frankness - "I'll tell you what it is, you're getting much the worst of the bargain!"

"We can only leave that for time to tell, Molly," drawing the girl to her with a tender kiss; "and now, Mary Olmstead Macon, I formally claim you as my own dear daughter; will it be hard for you to call me mother?"

"Not hard, but strange, dear Mrs. - mother -" blushing vividly; then, throwing her arms about the lady's neck with all the abandon she would have shown to Sara, she said heartily, "No, it isn't hard, dear, sweet mother, for I'm going to love you with all my heart!" and Mrs. Macon held her close, with a new fondness, born of possession, thrilling all her being.

After this there was no question but that Sara should be married from this new home, as both the professor and his wife insisted upon it; and when she tried to speak of paying board, Mrs. Macon only laughed at her.

"Now, Sara, do be quiet!" she said. "You may go on helping Henry till you get his new assistant broken in, of course - I won't say a word against that - but you must have every cent for your *trousseau* - and we'll show the madame some things that will make her open even her French eyes, I imagine!" this outburst having been called out by the receipt of a letter from the little woman that very morning.

Though it was one of warm approval and hearty good wishes, Mrs. Macon fancied she could read, between the lines of charming French-English, a desire to take the direction of affairs as soon as her husband's already improved condition should permit; and this did not suit the energetic manageress of this new family at all.

She had never been so much in her element for years. She delighted in life, stir, youth, and business; she liked to direct people - and, fortunately, Sara was one who could take even interference sweetly. So she arranged shopping tours, made engagements with dressmakers and milliners, and matched silk and lace with the greatest gusto, Sara being occasionally allowed a word in the matter.

Sometimes the latter attempted a remonstrance.

"But, Mrs. Macon," she whispered once, in alarm, "aren't you ordering more than I need of that silk? I'm afraid" -

"Now, my dear, I'm not going to have your dress spoiled for the lack of a yard or two. It's all fixed, and the clerk under-stands - and see here, don't be buying thread and linings, and such things - I've more than enough at home, so don't let's clutter ourselves with useless articles."

It was of no use to remonstrate - Marian Macon always had her way - and, if Sara would have honestly preferred a less expensive outfit, entirely of her own purchasing, she felt that it was little enough to do to sacrifice her well-loved independence to the generous whims of so kind and true a friend.

Miss Prue's answer to Sara's letter, announcing her

Fannie E. Newberry

engagement, was prompt and characteristic. She wished her every happiness, and was enthusiastic over Molly's good-fortune, but she could not help one little outburst.

"I did think you loved the sea, and your own people, too well to leave us forever - but I see it is not so - and I must say you've turned all my plans topsy-turvy! But perhaps, if you'll come down, and talk it over with me, I can bring myself to forgive you. Do come, Sara! If you go so far away, I may never see you again; for Polly and I are getting older, and more set in our ways, every day."

"I must go," she said to Mrs. Macon, reading part of the letter aloud, "if only for a few days; perhaps, too, I can then make some definite arrangement in regard to our cottage - how I do wish I could find a purchaser for it!"

She had expected to take the stage around the long way from Norcross to Killamet; but when she descended from the train what was her pleased surprise to be greeted by Bertha and - of all people - Jasper! They informed her they had rowed across the bay on purpose to take her home.

She tried not to feel embarrassed in the latter's presence, and wondered how much he knew of her plans; but Bertha was so bright and full of talk that there was little space for confusion or wonderings.

"How well you're looking, Bertha!" she said, as - now in the boat - Jasper pulled out from the sleepy little wharf. "You are as brown and rosy as any fisher-girl of us all."

As she spoke, half-idly, her glance taking in both figures before her, she could almost have sworn that a lightning-like eye-signal passed between them, before Bertha answered, with a conscious little laugh, -

"Well, I enjoy the life as if I had been born to it. Do you know, I can row - yes, and swim - as well as anybody, and I know all your old nooks, and" -

She paused suddenly, and Sara cried, -

"All mine? Why, who told you? Some of them you could never have found, I'm sure."

Bertha blushed, but Jasper spoke up bravely, -

"Oh, I showed her. She's a great climber as you used to be, Sairay."

"That was nice of you, Jasper! So you know the 'Mermaid's Castle,' and the pine walk, and all?"

Bertha assented, then turned the subject to Mrs. Searle, the cottage, etc., while Sara began to have a dawning feeling that, possibly, she need not worry over Jasper's future happiness, at least to the exclusion of her own.

Miss Prue greeted her warmly; and everything was so exactly the same, from the white, curving beach, and long fish-sheds, the unpainted houses and the plants in the bow-windows, to the red and green carpet, and dragon-china in her little parlor, that Sara could hardly believe she had ever been away. Hester, seemingly not a day older, and wearing the identical turban she had last seen her in, Sara felt certain, greeted her with respectful warmth, and Polly grunted, -

"Come in - shut the door - how d'ye do? - Git out!" in her old familiar style.

Jasper had come with her to the door to carry the large valise, which was the only luggage she had brought; but Bertha bade them *au revoir* at the turn, saying she must hurry back to Mrs. Searle.

"Won't you come in and stay to supper, Jasper?" asked Miss Prue, as he set the valise down and prepared to depart.

"No, thank you, Cousin Prue, I've got some marketing to take home to mother that she sent for to Norcross."

"Well, come down this evening, then."

"Guess I will, thank you. I told Bertha I'd call around after her - she'd like to come too."

"Humph! very well," said his cousin, closing the door after him with more vim than was strictly necessary.

"How good it seems to be here once more!" exclaimed Sara, looking all about her. "You've had a new set of book-shelves put in, haven't you? That's all the change I see."

"Yes, and all you'll find in the whole village, likely, except in your own house - that you'd never know."

"Have you made acquaintance with Mrs. Searle and Bertha?" asked Sara, after Miss Prue had returned from trotting away with her wraps. "Oh, yes; she's a nice woman when she isn't under the dominion of her nerves, and she says she hasn't been so well in years as she is here; the air seems to agree with her, and she enjoys the quiet."

"I'm glad of that. How do you like Bertha?"

"Oh, she's a nice girl," carelessly; "she thinks the world of you."

"Does she?" smiling a little; "it's mutual."

Then her hostess asked after the twins, the Macons, etc., after which they went out to supper.

In the evening Bertha came with Jasper. There was an abounding joyousness in her manner, which so tallied with Sara's deep happiness that she could not but notice it; and it was evident that there was at least perfect good feeling, if nothing more, between her and Jasper.

After they had gone, Sara turned with a mischievous look to her old friend.

"I've an idea, Miss Prue, that Bertha is quite in love with - Killamet and its environs; she seems really enthusiastic. But how does it happen that Jasper is at home now?"

"Well, the season is nearly over, and I believe his schooner is undergoing repairs - he's his own master now, and goes and comes as he likes."

"Yes; that must be pleasant! He seems unusually well; I never saw him looking so handsome."

"Humph!" said Miss Prue, and drew the curtain sharply, after which they adjourned for the night.

Sara found Miss Prue was right about her own house. Two coats of paint outside gave it a decidedly spruce appearance, while, inside, that lady's vision as to its capabilities had been more than realized. The blending of roughness and luxury, of camp and home characteristics, gave the large central apartment a quaintness that had real charm for eyes weary of too great sameness in house-decoration; and when Mrs. Searle began negotiations for buying the place, Sara felt, for a moment, very loath to sell. But she quickly conquered the feeling, knowing its uselessness; and as the purchaser was in real earnest, and no haggler, while the seller had not an idea how to drive a hard bargain, they soon came to terms satisfactory to both.

As Mrs. Searle held out her feeble hand from her invalid chair to bid Sara farewell, she retained the young girl's a moment to say, -

"You will not mind an old woman's congratulating you upon your future, will you? I knew Robert Glendenning's father in

Fannie E. Newberry

my youth; and if the son is like him in character, you may well be congratulated."

Sara blushingly murmured her acknowledgments, and the lady continued, -

"I want to thank you for sending me Bertha, also; she's a real little treasure."

"I'm so glad you like each other, Mrs. Searle! Do you know, that whole affair has always seemed providential to me? I was a passive instrument in wiser hands." "As we all are, more often than we think - well, good-by, and when you long for a sight of the old home, and the sea, you will always be welcome here."

It was Sara's only visit to the cottage, for her stay in Killamet was necessarily short. She spent all the time possible with her dear old friend, who she could plainly see, was losing in vigor daily. But though she frankly referred to her approaching marriage, and discussed her future plans in detail, it was not till the last day that either touched upon the subject as affecting Jasper.

He had sailed away that morning, bidding her a kind farewell, but reserving his last look and handclasp for Bertha; and as the two girls walked back together from the beach, stopping to call on Zeba Osterhaus and Mrs. Updyke by the way, she could but notice how quiet her friend seemed, and mentioned it later to Miss Prue, with the bold comment, -

"She will miss Jasper greatly, for, as I understand, they have been together almost constantly these last two months."

Her hostess knitted a round or two before she answered.

"Well, and I suppose you think that shows conclusively that he never cared anything for you - but it doesn't. Jasper's as steady and faithful as the sun, and if you had married him he would have been a loyal husband to his dying day. But you wouldn't. At least that's my explanation of matters; I know he went down to Norcross on business, and came home looking as if he had buried all his friends. He acknowledged he had seen you, and it didn't take me long to figure out the matter - and, Sara Olmstead, I will own I was disappointed in you - dreadfully disappointed! He met Bertha right here at my house - happened in one day when she was here on an errand - and she said something pleasant about you. That caught his attention, and I really believe, for a while, he sought that girl out just to hear her praises of you; and if it has grown to be something different with time, you ought to be the last one to blame him."

"Blame him? My dear Miss Prue, I think it's the nicest thing in the world - only, I came down here, you know, on purpose to win your forgiveness, and I'm not willing to go back without it."

"Oh, of course you'll get it - you know that - but I've got to go and plan out a whole new will, for I had determined to leave everything equally divided between you and Jasper which I can't do now without splitting everything in two, so" -

"I'm to be cut off with a shilling?" gayly; "but I won't complain, if you'll only continue to give me your love - ah! dear Miss Prue, I am mercenary in one way, only - I do want all the affection I can beg or borrow!"

For answer, the elder maiden took the younger in her arms and gave her a most tender kiss - so peace was made, and the ambassador who had failed to bring about the nuptials so ardently desired was at last propitiated.

This time it was old Adam Standish who rowed Sara over the bay to Norcross, - Adam, unchanged in lineament or costume, - while faithful friends, as before, watched from the beach. Again she looked back with tear-dimmed eyes; for tender memories of father, mother, baby-brother, and all childhood's

Fannie E. Newberry

associations, tugged at her heart-strings - but there was now no dread and fear to paralyze her.

She faced an uncertain future, it is true, but one bounded by tenderness and care, whose horizon-line glowed before her with rosy visions, which stretched away in glad promise to the infinite deeps of Heaven!

Choose from Thousands of 1stWorldLibrary Classics By

A. M. Barnard
Ada Leverson
Adolphus William Ward
Aesop
Agatha Christie
Alexander Aaronsohn
Alexander Kielland
Alexandre Dumas
Alfred Gatty
Alfred Ollivant
Alice Duer Miller
Alice Turner Curtis
Alice Dunbar
Allen Chapman
Ambrose Bierce
Amelia E. Barr
Amory H. Bradford
Andrew Lang
Andrew McFarland Davis
Andy Adams
Anna Alice Chapin
Anna Sewell
Annie Besant
Annie Hamilton Donnell
Annie Payson Call
Annie Roe Carr
Annonaymous
Anton Chekhov
Arnold Bennett
Arthur Conan Doyle
Arthur M. Winfield
Arthur Ransome
Arthur Schnitzler
Atticus
B.H. Baden-Powell
B. M. Bower
B. C. Chatterjee
Baroness Emmuska Orczy
Baroness Orczy
Basil King
Bayard Taylor
Ben Macomber
Bertha Muzzy Bower
Bjornstjerne Bjornson
Booth Tarkington
Boyd Cable
Bram Stoker
C. Collodi
C. E. Orr

C. M. Ingleby
Carolyn Wells
Catherine Parr Traill
Charles A. Eastman
Charles Amory Beach
Charles Dickens
Charles Dudley Warner
Charles Farrar Browne
Charles Ives
Charles Kingsley
Charles Klein
Charles Hanson Towne
Charles Lathrop Pack
Charles Romyn Dake
Charles Whibley
Charles Willing Beale
Charlotte M. Braeme
Charlotte M. Yonge
Charlotte Perkins Stetson
Clair W. Hayes
Clarence Day Jr.
Clarence E. Mulford
Clemence Housman
Confucius
Coningsby Dawson
Cornelis DeWitt Wilcox
Cyril Burleigh
D. H. Lawrence
Daniel Defoe
David Garnett
Dinah Craik
Don Carlos Janes
Donald Keyhoe
Dorothy Kilner
Dougan Clark
Douglas Fairbanks
E. Nesbit
E.P.Roe
E. Phillips Oppenheim
Earl Barnes
Edgar Rice Burroughs
Edith Van Dyne
Edith Wharton
Edward Everett Hale
Edward J. O'Biren
Edward S. Ellis
Edwin L. Arnold
Eleanor Atkins
Eliot Gregory

Elizabeth Gaskell
Elizabeth McCracken
Elizabeth Von Arnim
Ellem Key
Emerson Hough
Emilie F. Carlen
Emily Dickinson
Enid Bagnold
Enilor Macartney Lane
Erasmus W. Jones
Ernie Howard Pie
Ethel May Dell
Ethel Turner
Ethel Watts Mumford
Eugenie Foa
Eugene Wood
Eustace Hale Ball
Evelyn Everett-green
Everard Cotes
F. H. Cheley
F. J. Cross
F. Marion Crawford
Federick Austin Ogg
Ferdinand Ossendowski
Francis Bacon
Francis Darwin
Frances Hodgson Burnett
Frances Parkinson Keyes
Frank Gee Patchin
Frank Harris
Frank Jewett Mather
Frank L. Packard
Frank V. Webster
Frederic Stewart Isham
Frederick Trevor Hill
Frederick Winslow Taylor
Friedrich Kerst
Friedrich Nietzsche
Fyodor Dostoyevsky
G.A. Henty
G.K. Chesterton
Gabrielle E. Jackson
Garrett P. Serviss
Gaston Leroux
George A. Warren
George Ade
Geroge Bernard Shaw
George Durston
George Ebers

George Eliot
George Gissing
George MacDonald
George Meredith
George Orwell
George Sylvester Viereck
George Tucker
George W. Cable
George Wharton James
Gertrude Atherton
Gordon Casserly
Grace E. King
Grace Gallatin
Grace Greenwood
Grant Allen
Guillermo A. Sherwell
Gulielma Zollinger
Gustav Flaubert
H. A. Cody
H. B. Irving
H.C. Bailey
H. G. Wells
H. H. Munro
H. Irving Hancock
H. Rider Haggard
H. W. C. Davis
Haldeman Julius
Hall Caine
Hamilton Wright Mabie
Hans Christian Andersen
Harold Avery
Harold McGrath
Harriet Beecher Stowe
Harry Castlemon
Harry Coghill
Harry Houidini
Hayden Carruth
Helent Hunt Jackson
Helen Nicolay
Hendrik Conscience
Hendy David Thoreau
Henri Barbusse
Henrik Ibsen
Henry Adams
Henry Ford
Henry Frost
Henry James
Henry Jones Ford
Henry Seton Merriman
Henry W Longfellow
Herbert A. Giles

Herbert Carter
Herbert N. Casson
Herman Hesse
Hildegard G. Frey
Homer
Honore De Balzac
Horace B. Day
Horace Walpole
Horatio Alger Jr.
Howard Pyle
Howard R. Garis
Hugh Lofting
Hugh Walpole
Humphry Ward
Ian Maclaren
Inez Haynes Gillmore
Irving Bacheller
Isabel Hornibrook
Israel Abrahams
Ivan Turgenev
J.G.Austin
J. Henri Fabre
J. M. Barrie
J. Macdonald Oxley
J. S. Fletcher
J. S. Knowles
J. Storer Clouston
Jack London
Jacob Abbott
James Allen
James Andrews
James Baldwin
James Branch Cabell
James DeMille
James Joyce
James Lane Allen
James Lane Allen
James Oliver Curwood
James Oppenheim
James Otis
James R. Driscoll
Jane Austen
Jane L. Stewart
Janet Aldridge
Jens Peter Jacobsen
Jerome K. Jerome
John Burroughs
John Cournos
John F. Kennedy
John Gay
John Glasworthy

John Habberton
John Joy Bell
John Kendrick Bangs
John Milton
John Philip Sousa
Jonas Lauritz Idemil Lie
Jonathan Swift
Joseph A. Altsheler
Joseph Carey
Joseph Conrad
Joseph E. Badger Jr
Joseph Hergesheimer
Joseph Jacobs
Jules Vernes
Julian Hawthrone
Julie A Lippmann
Justin Huntly McCarthy
Kakuzo Okakura
Kenneth Grahame
Kenneth McGaffey
Kate Langley Bosher
Kate Langley Bosher
Katherine Cecil Thurston
Katherine Stokes
L. A. Abbot
L. T. Meade
L. Frank Baum
Latta Griswold
Laura Dent Crane
Laura Lee Hope
Laurence Housman
Lawrence Beasley
Leo Tolstoy
Leonid Andreyev
Lewis Carroll
Lewis Sperry Chafer
Lilian Bell
Lloyd Osbourne
Louis Hughes
Louis Tracy
Louisa May Alcott
Lucy Fitch Perkins
Lucy Maud Montgomery
Luther Benson
Lydia Miller Middleton
Lyndon Orr
M. Corvus
M. H. Adams
Margaret E. Sangster
Margret Howth
Margaret Vandercook

Margret Penrose
Maria Edgeworth
Maria Thompson Daviess
Mariano Azuela
Marion Polk Angellotti
Mark Overton
Mark Twain
Mary Austin
Mary Catherine Crowley
Mary Cole
Mary Hastings Bradley
Mary Roberts Rinehart
Mary Rowlandson
M. Wollstonecraft Shelley
Maud Lindsay
Max Beerbohm
Myra Kelly
Nathaniel Hawthrone
Nicolo Machiavelli
O. F. Walton
Oscar Wilde
Owen Johnson
P.G. Wodehouse
Paul and Mabel Thorne
Paul G. Tomlinson
Paul Severing
Percy Brebner
Peter B. Kyne
Plato
R. Derby Holmes
R. L. Stevenson
R. S. Ball
Rabindranath Tagore
Rahul Alvares
Ralph Bonehill
Ralph Henry Barbour
Ralph Victor
Ralph Waldo Emmerson
Rene Descartes
Rex Beach

Rex E. Beach
Richard Harding Davis
Richard Jefferies
Richard Le Gallienne
Robert Barr
Robert Frost
Robert Gordon Anderson
Robert L. Drake
Robert Lansing
Robert Lynd
Robert Michael Ballantyne
Robert W. Chambers
Rosa Nouchette Carey
Rudyard Kipling
Samuel B. Allison
Samuel Hopkins Adams
Sarah Bernhardt
Sarah C. Hallowell
Selma Lagerlof
Sherwood Anderson
Sigmund Freud
Standish O'Grady
Stanley Weyman
Stella Benson
Stella M. Francis
Stephen Crane
Stewart Edward White
Stijn Streuvels
Swami Abhedananda
Swami Parmananda
T. S. Ackland
T. S. Arthur
The Princess Der Ling
Thomas A. Janvier
Thomas A Kempis
Thomas Anderton
Thomas Bailey Aldrich
Thomas Bulfinch
Thomas De Quincey
Thomas Dixon

Thomas H. Huxley
Thomas Hardy
Thomas More
Thornton W. Burgess
U. S. Grant
Valentine Williams
Various Authors
Vaughan Kester
Victor Appleton
Victoria Cross
Virginia Woolf
Wadsworth Camp
Walter Camp
Walter Scott
Washington Irving
Wilbur Lawton
Wilkie Collins
Willa Cather
Willard F. Baker
William Dean Howells
William le Queux
W. Makepeace Thackeray
William W. Walter
William Shakespeare
Winston Churchill
Yei Theodora Ozaki
Yogi Ramacharaka
Young E. Allison
Zane Grey